FOR ORGANS, PIANOS & ELECTRONIC KEYBOARDS

E-Z PLAY TODAY

400

CLASSICAL MASTERPIECES

T0034091

ISBN 978-0-634-01690-5

HAL•LEONARD® CORPORATION

7777 W. BLUEMOUND RD. P.O. BOX 13819 MILWAUKEE, WI 53213

Visit Hal Leonard Online at
www.halleonard.com

CLASSICAL MASTERPIECES

Air on the G String
from ORCHESTRAL SUITE NO. 3

Registration 10
Rhythm: None

By Johann Sebastian Bach

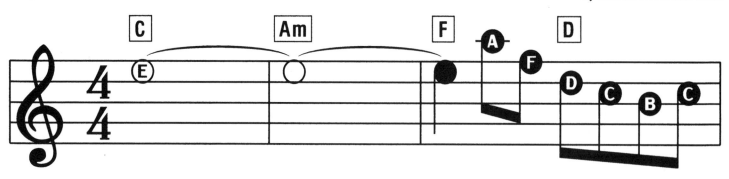

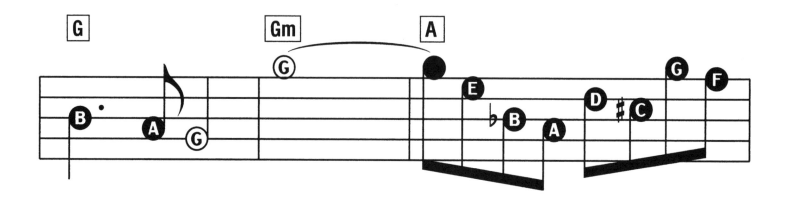

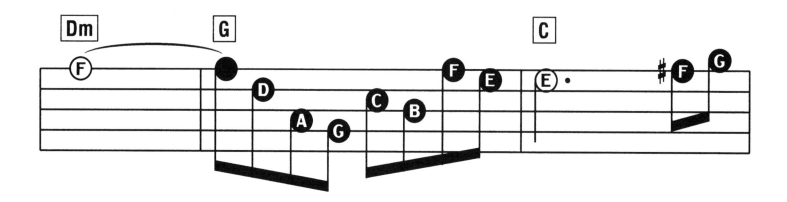

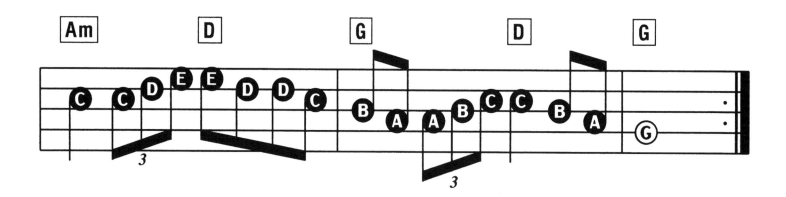

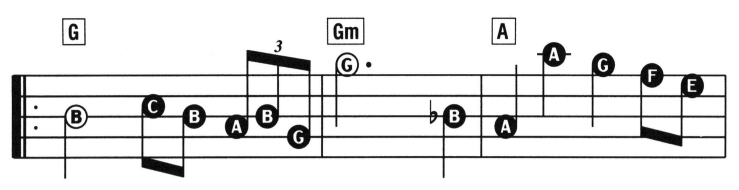

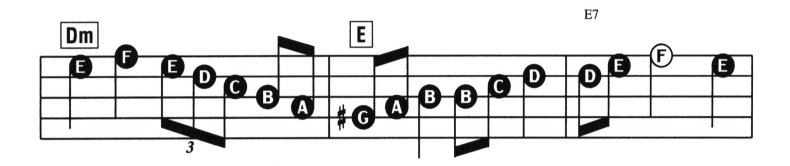

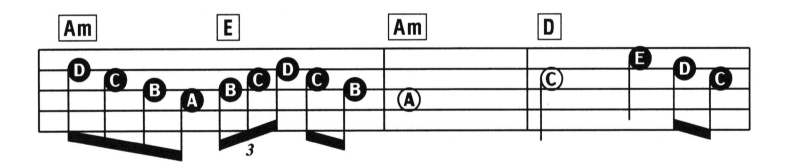

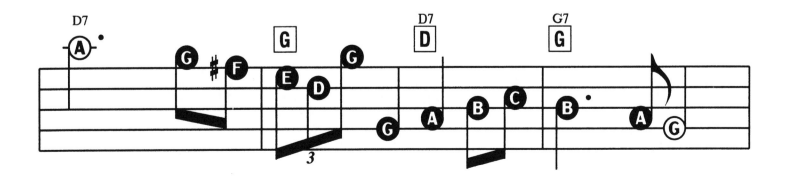

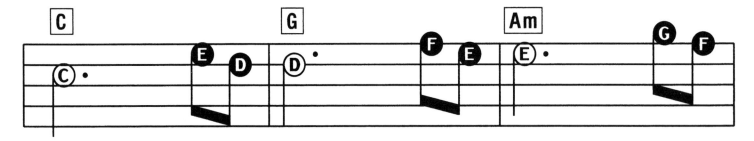

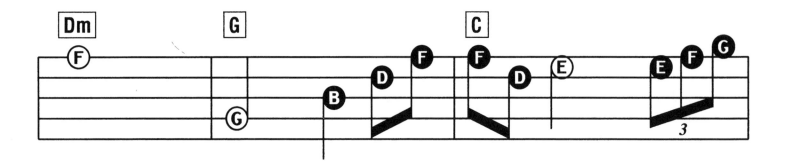

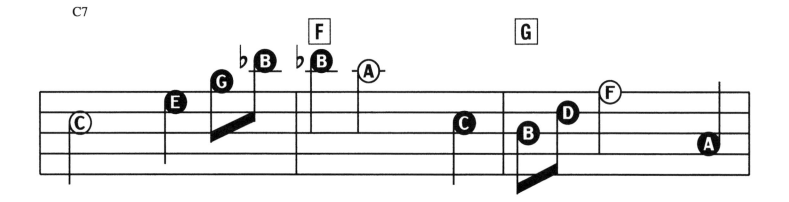

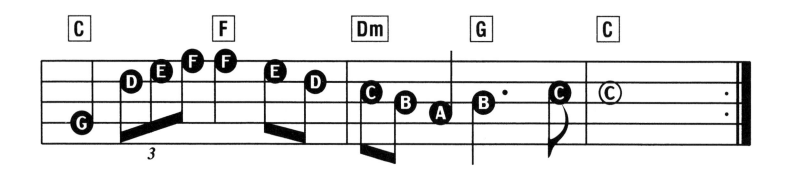

Alleluia
from EXSULTATE, JUBILATE

Registration 1
Rhythm: None

By Wolfgang Amadeus Mozart

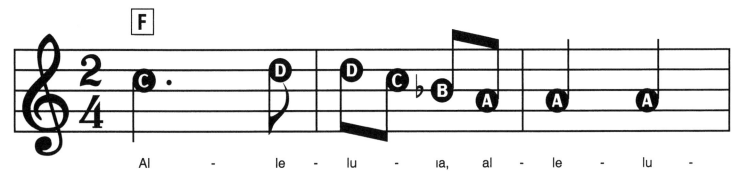

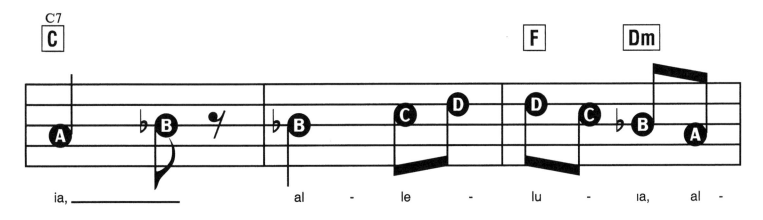

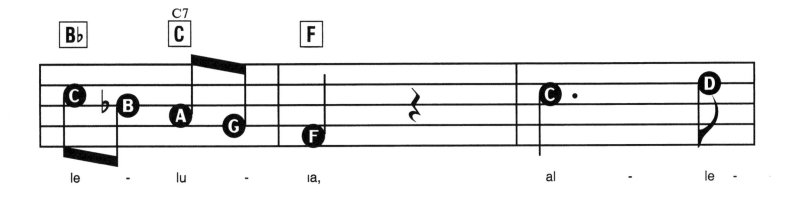

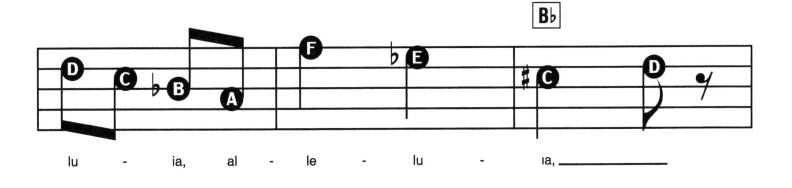

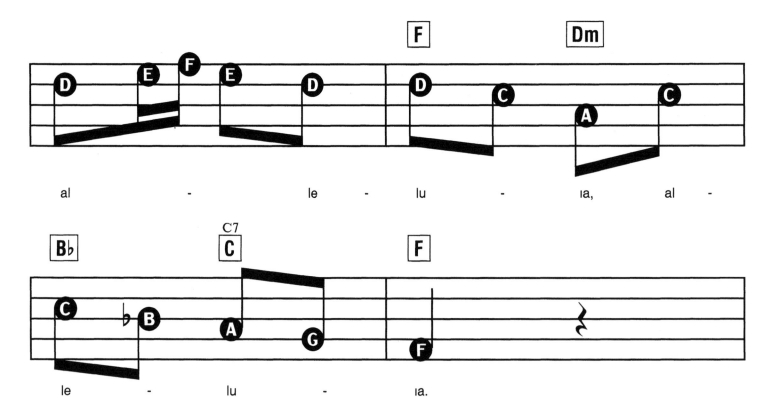

al - le - lu - ia, al -

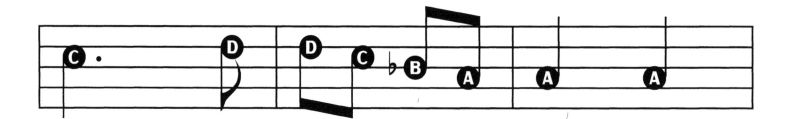

le - lu - ia.

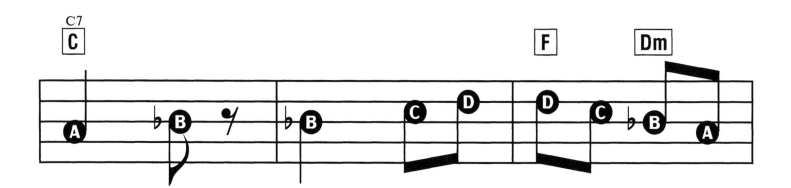

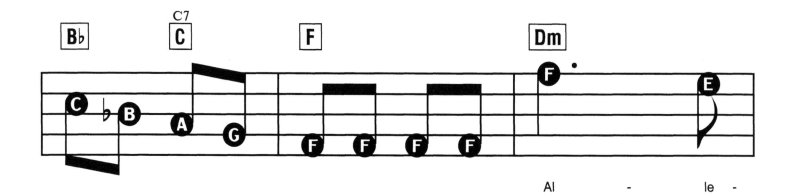

Al - le -

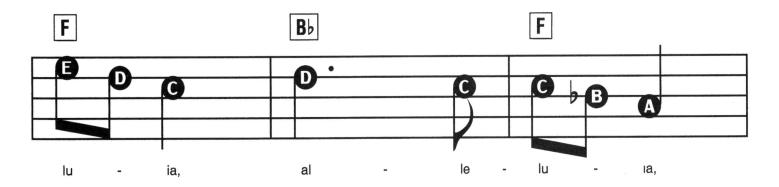

lu - ia, al - le - lu - ia,

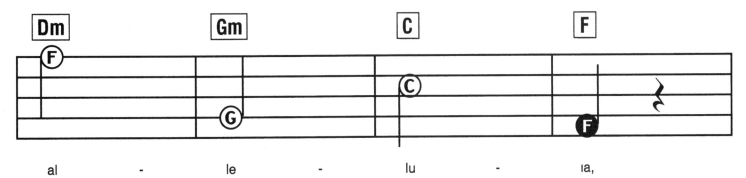

al - le - lu - ia,

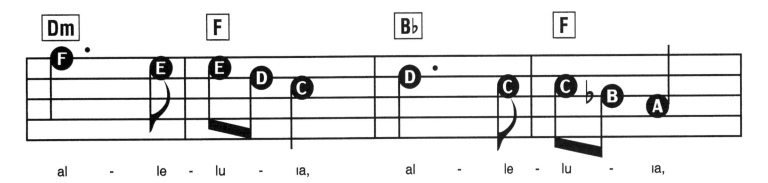

al - le - lu - ia, al - le - lu - ia,

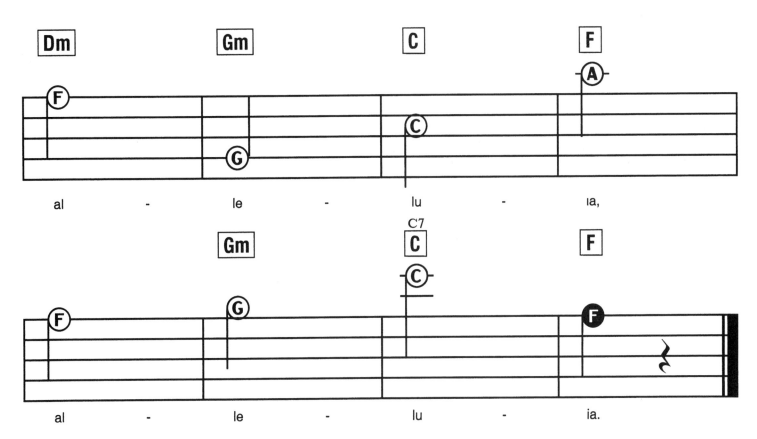

al - le - lu - ia,

al - le - lu - ia.

Allegro maestoso
from WATER MUSIC

Registration 4
Rhythm: None

By George Frideric Handel

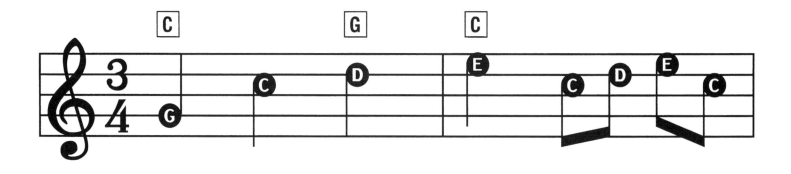

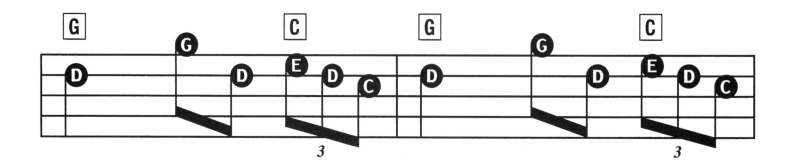

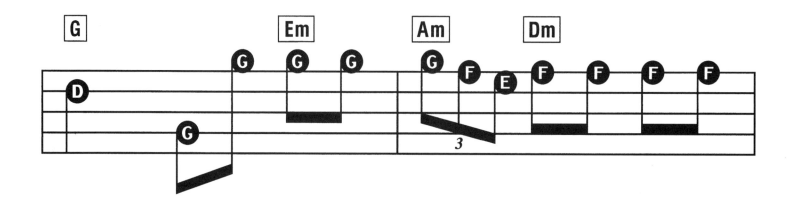

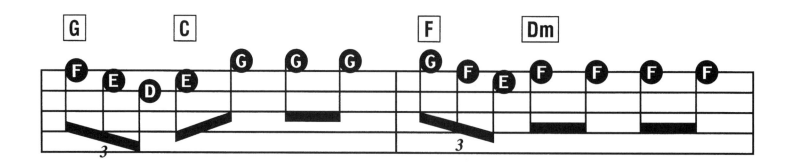

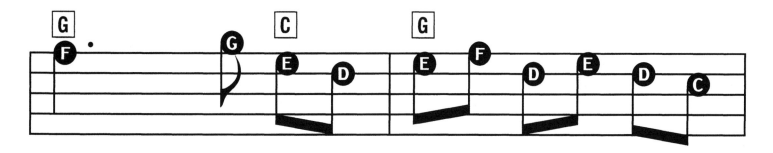

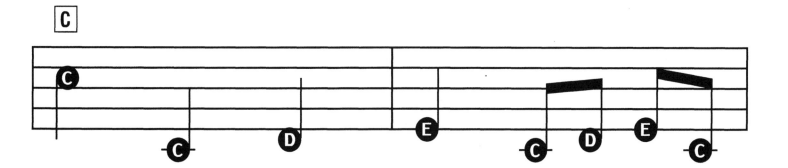

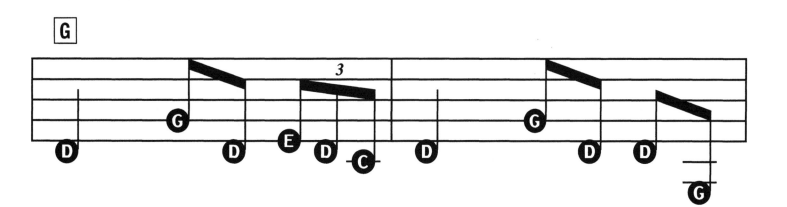

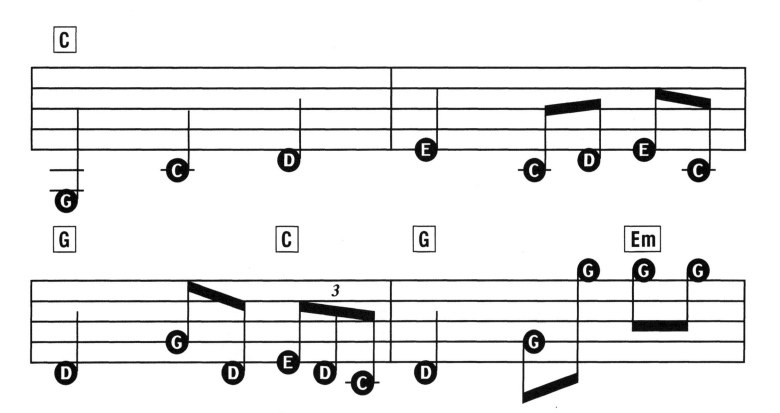

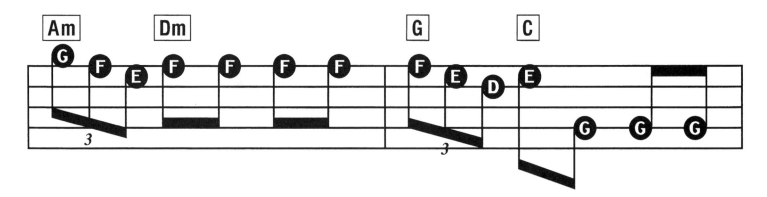

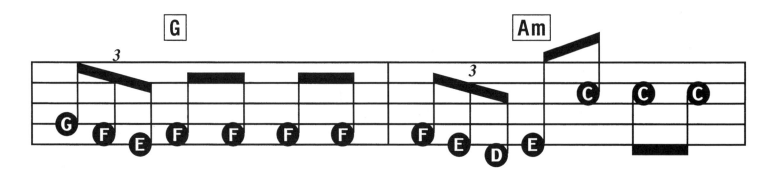

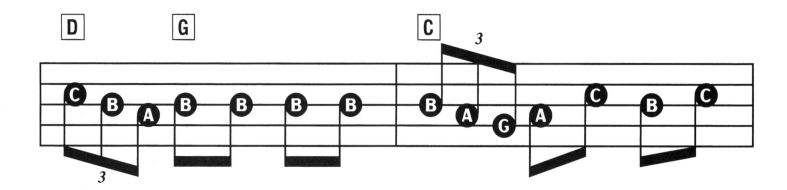

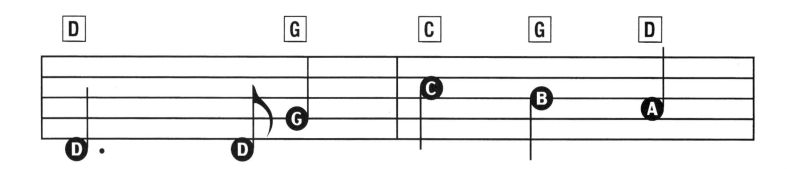

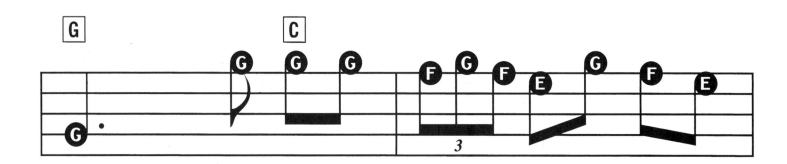

Only

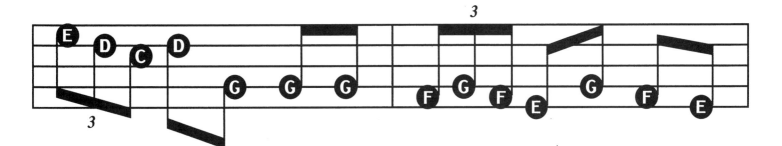

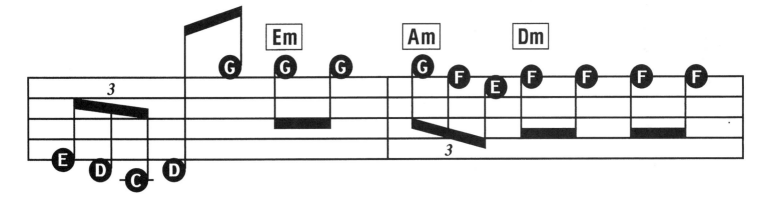

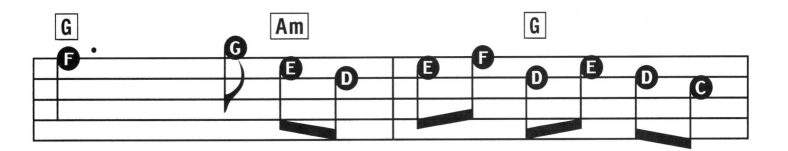

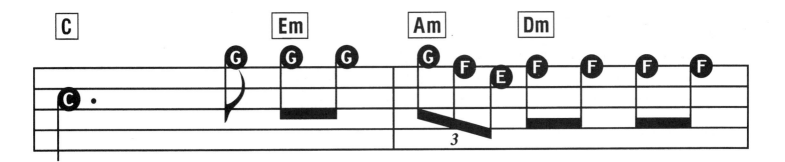

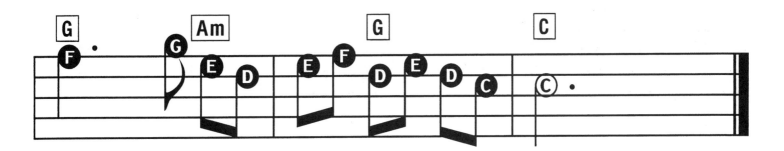

Anvil Chorus
from IL TROVATORE

Registration 4
Rhythm: March

By Giuseppe Verdi

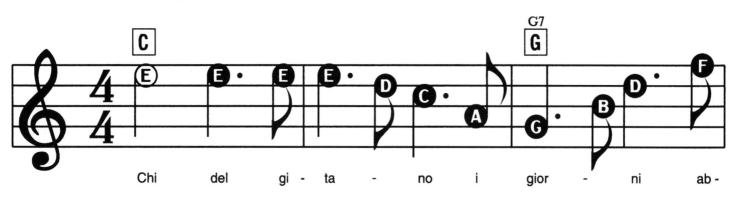

Chi del gi - ta - no i gior - ni ab -

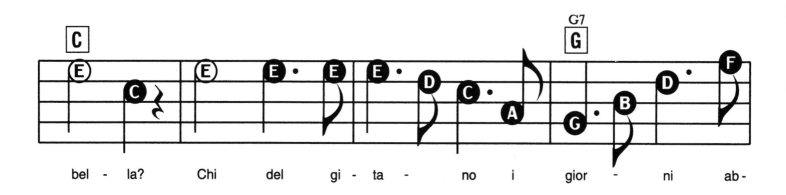

bel - la? Chi del gi - ta - no i gior - ni ab -

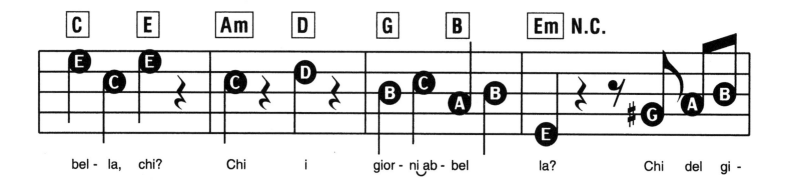

bel - la, chi? Chi i gior - ni ab - bel la? Chi del gi -

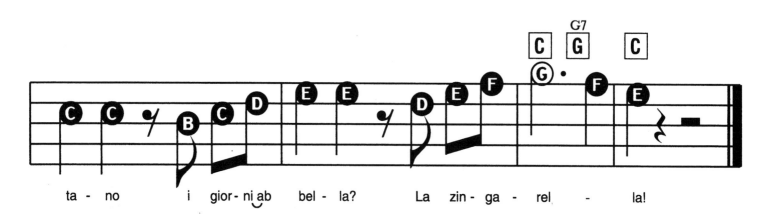

ta - no i gior - ni ab bel - la? La zin - ga - rel - la!

Ave Maria
based on Prelude in C by Johann Sebastian Bach

Registration 7
Rhythm: None

By Charles Gounod

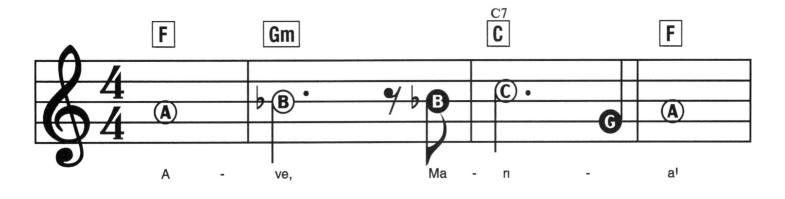

A - ve, Ma - ri - a!

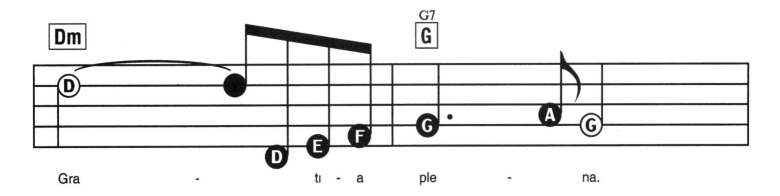

Gra - ti - a ple - na.

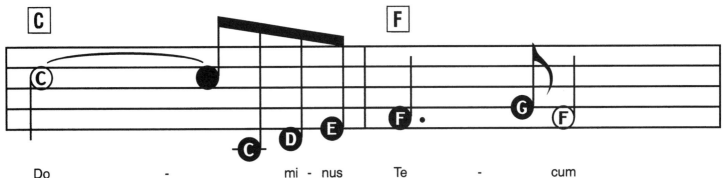

Do - mi - nus Te - cum

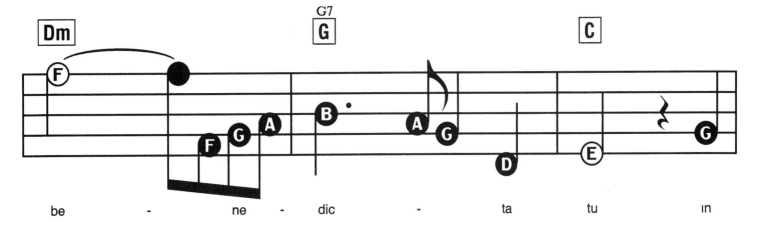

be - ne - dic - ta tu in

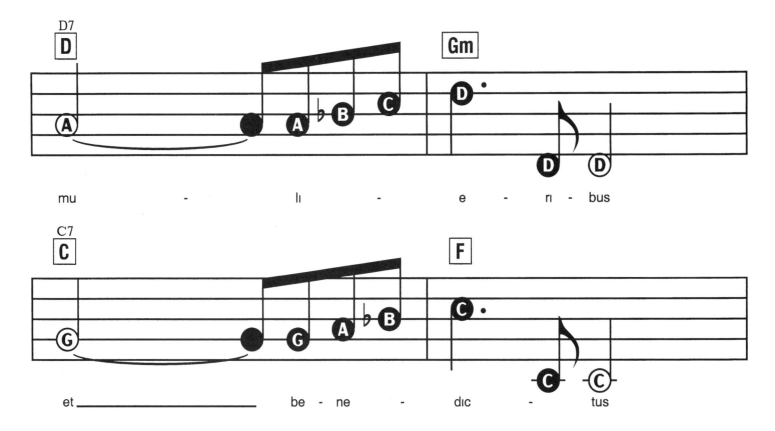

mu - li - e - ri - bus

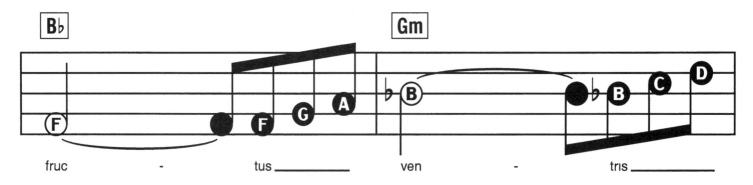

et _____ be - ne - dic - tus

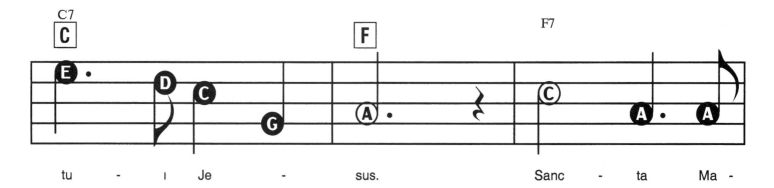

fruc - tus _____ ven - tris _____

tu - i Je - sus. Sanc - ta Ma -

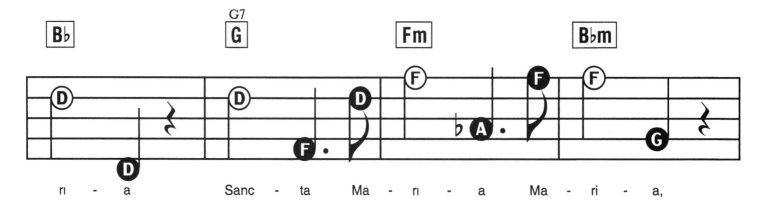

ri - a Sanc - ta Ma - ri - a Ma - ri - a,

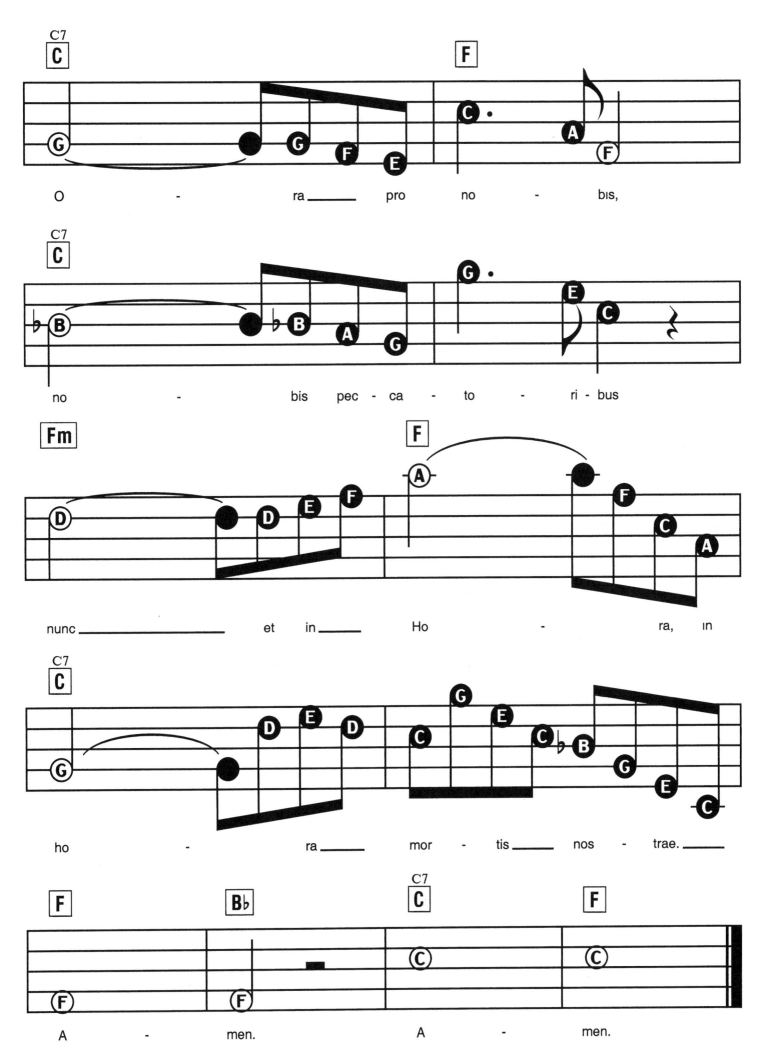

Arab Dance
from THE NUTCRACKER

Registration 2
Rhythm: None

By Pyotr Il'yich Tchaikovsky

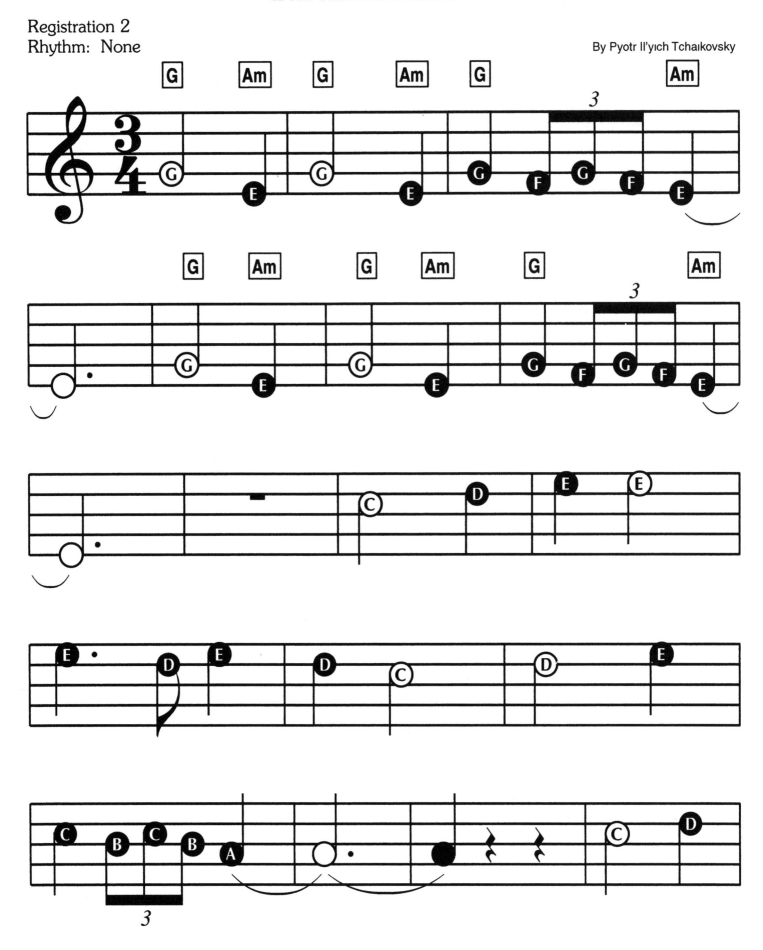

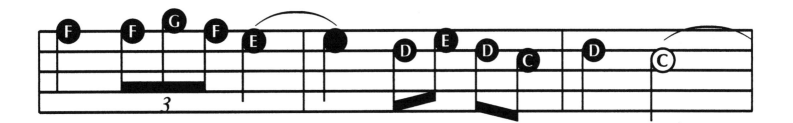

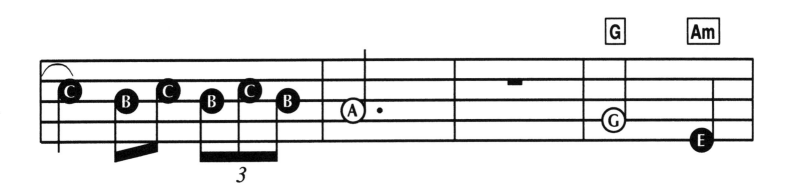

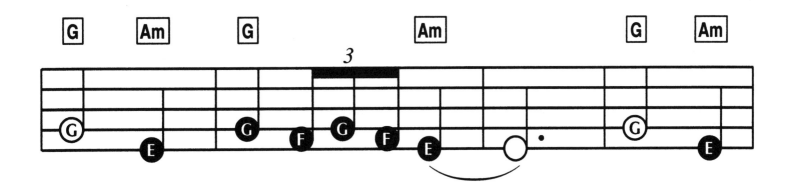

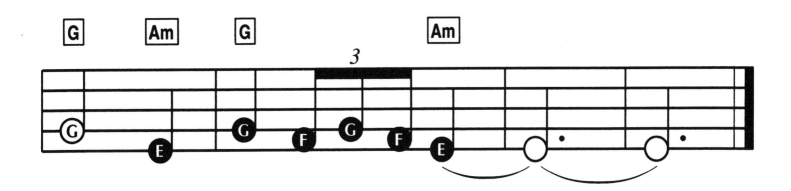

Barcarolle
from THE TALES OF HOFFMANN (LES CONTES D'HOFFMANN)

Registration 4
Rhythm: Waltz

By Jacques Offenbach

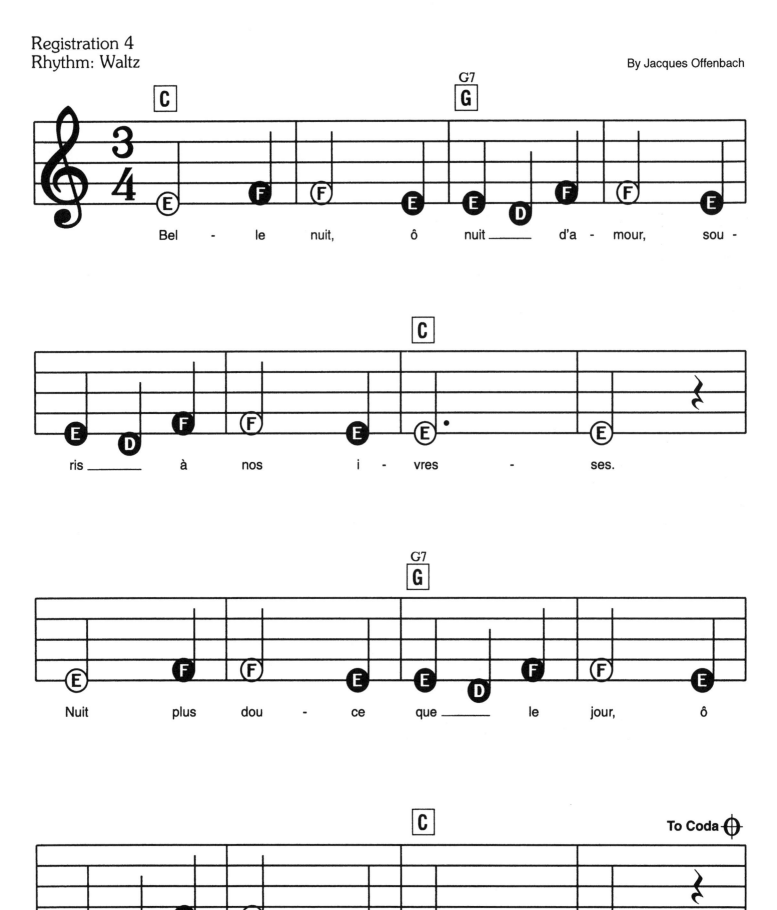

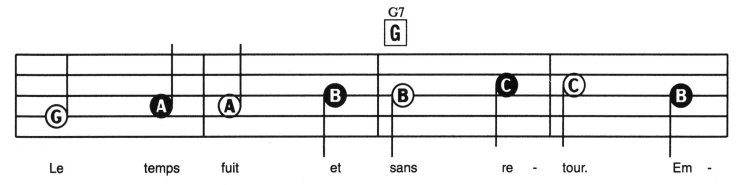

Le temps fuit et sans re - tour. Em -

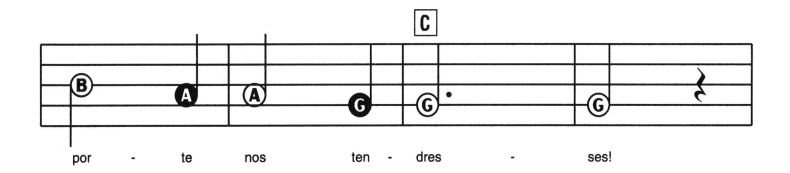

por - te nos ten - dres - ses!

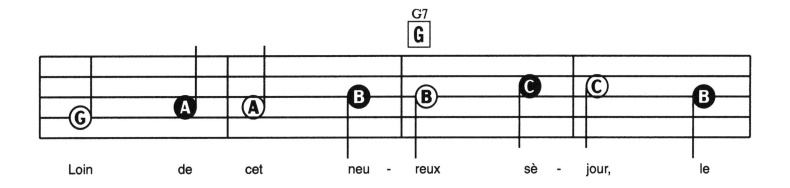

Loin de cet neu - reux sè - jour, le

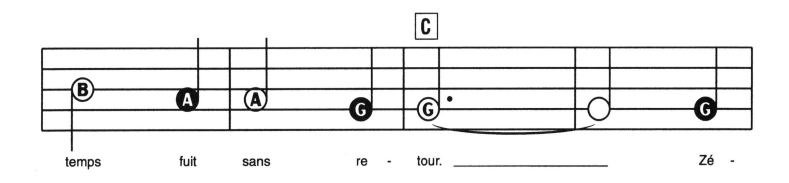

temps fuit sans re - tour. _____ Zé -

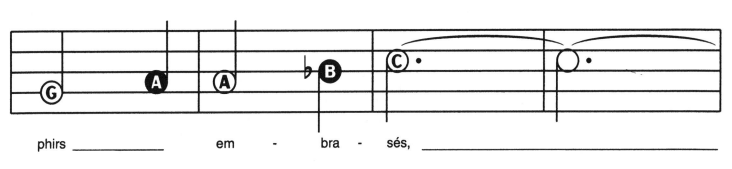

phirs _____ em - bra - sés, _____

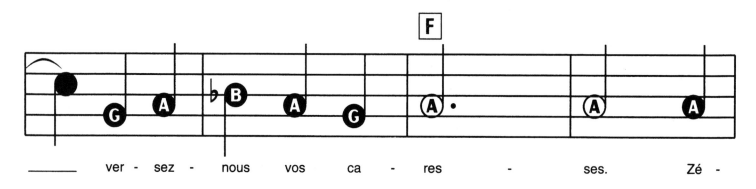

ver - sez - nous vos ca - res - ses. Zé -

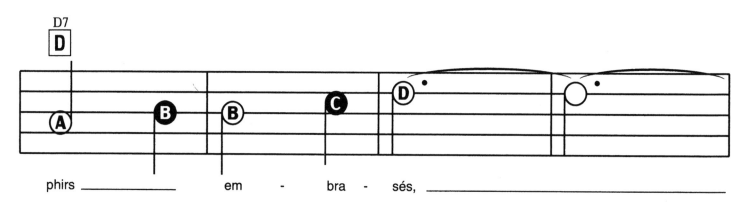

phirs em - bra - sés,

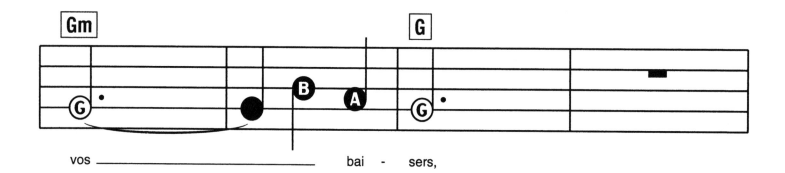

don - nez - nous vos bai - sers,

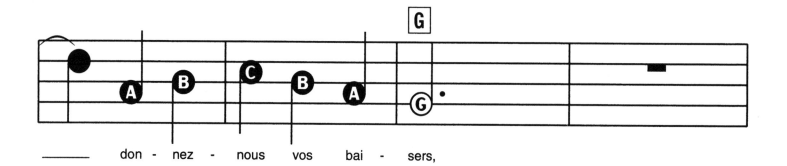

vos bai - sers,

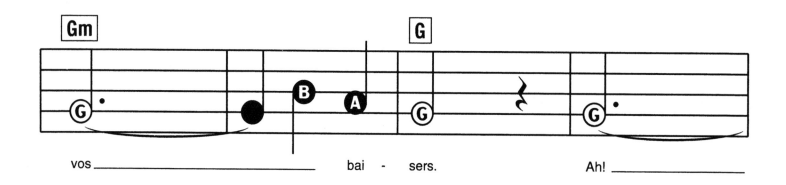

vos bai - sers. Ah!

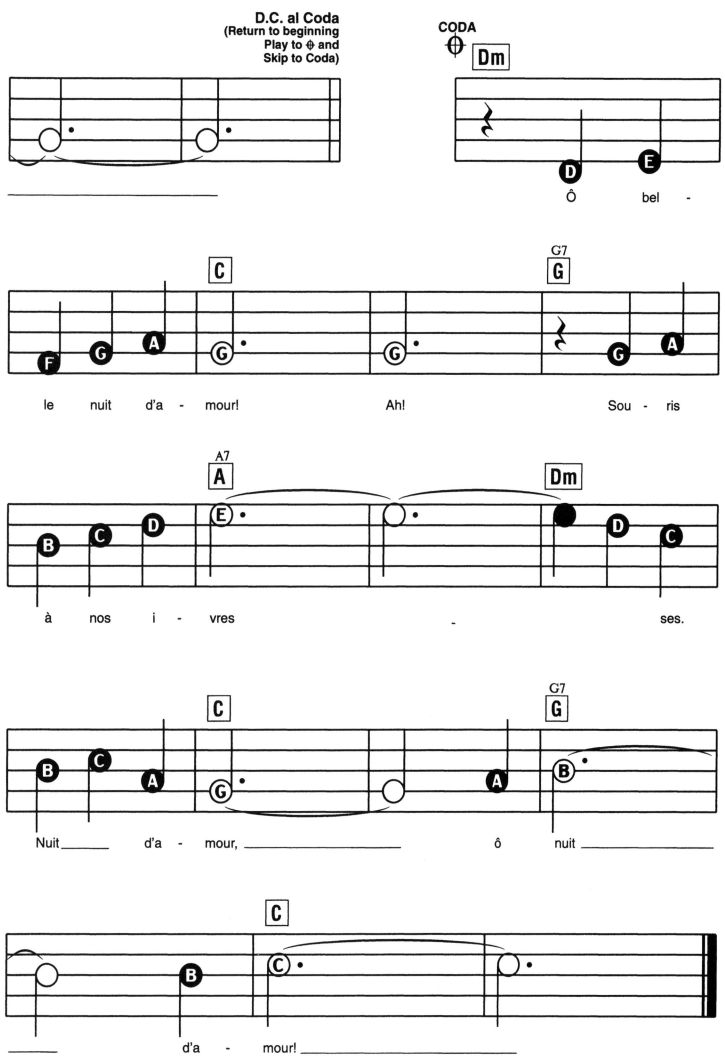

By the Beautiful Blue Danube

Registration 2
Rhythm: Waltz

By Johann Strauss, Jr

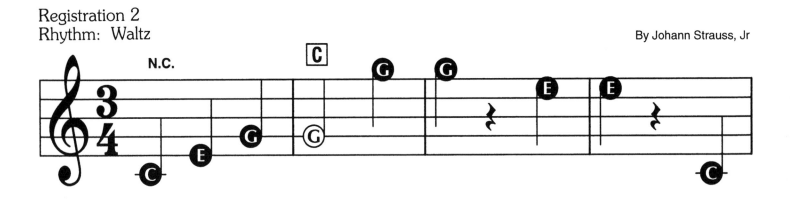

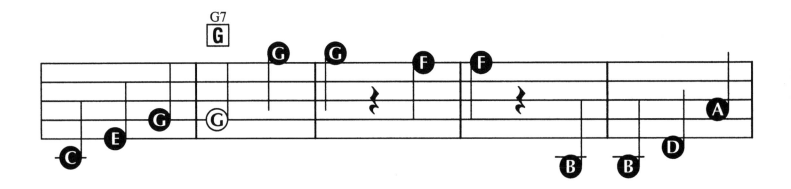

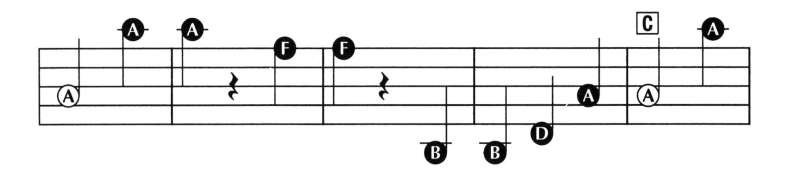

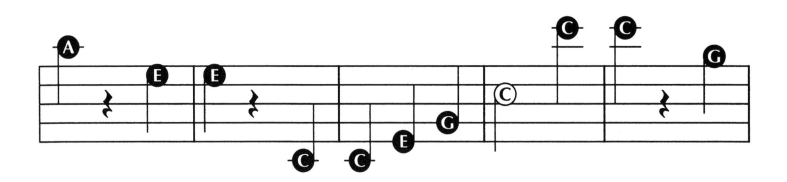

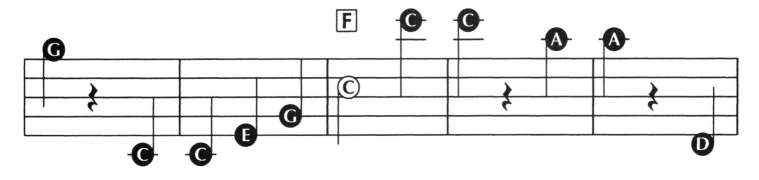

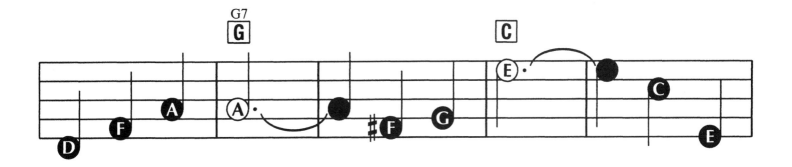

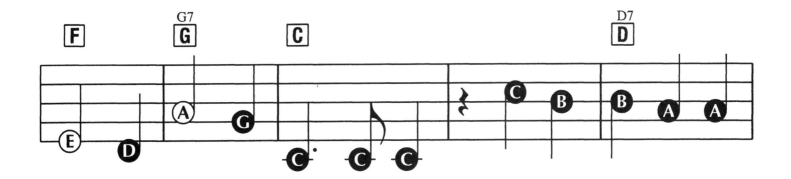

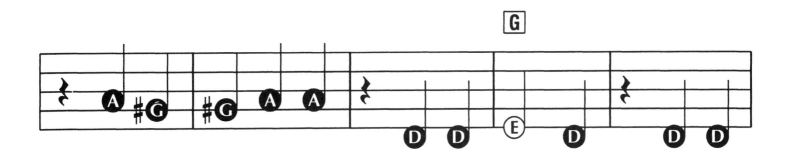

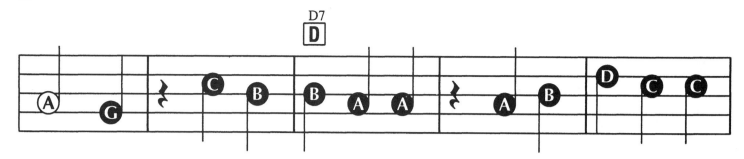

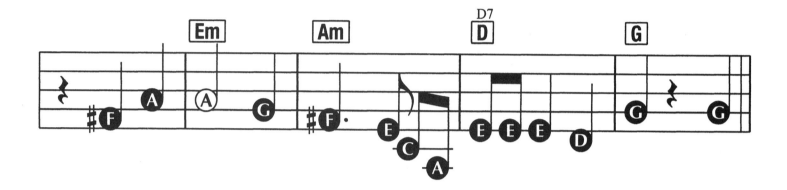

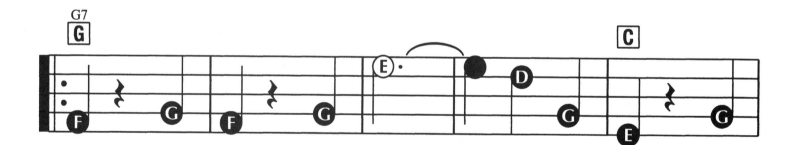

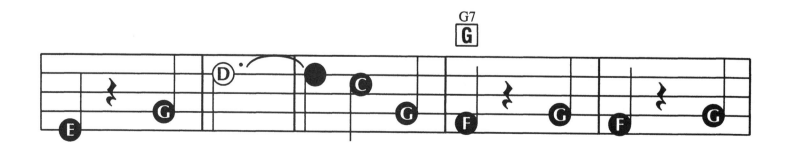

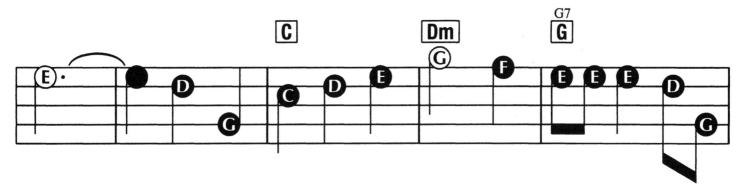

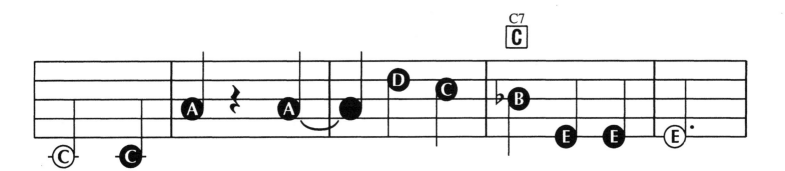

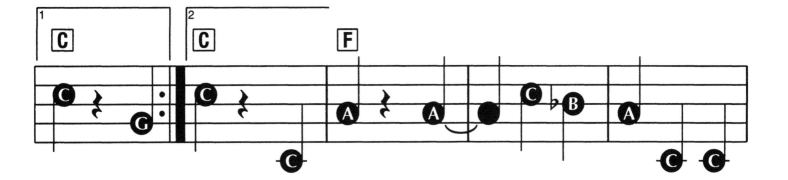

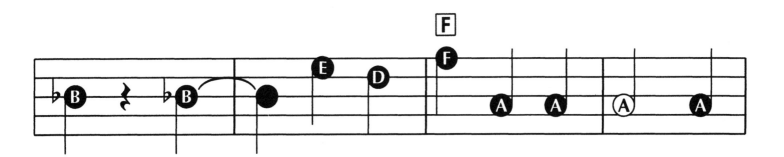

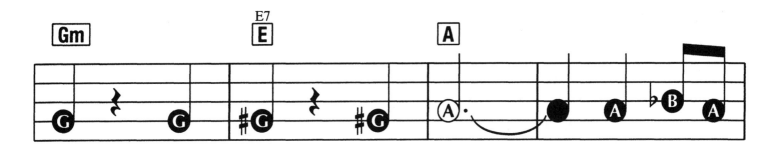

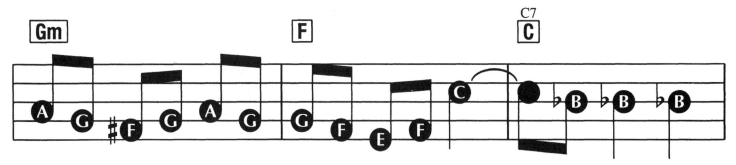

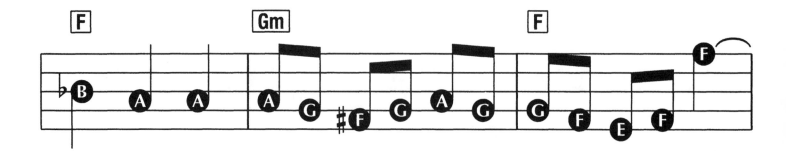

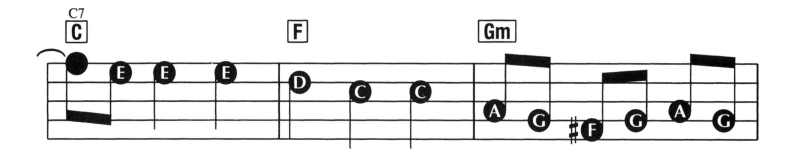

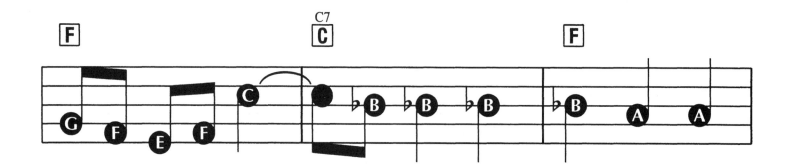

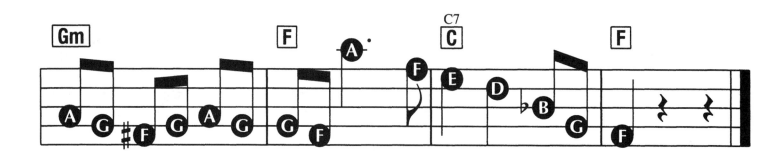

1812 Overture
Excerpt

Registration 2
Rhythm: March

By Pyotr Il'yich Tchaikovsky

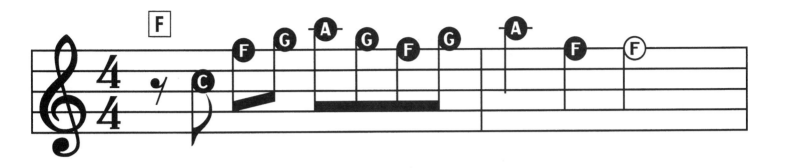

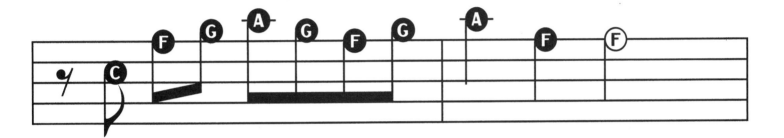

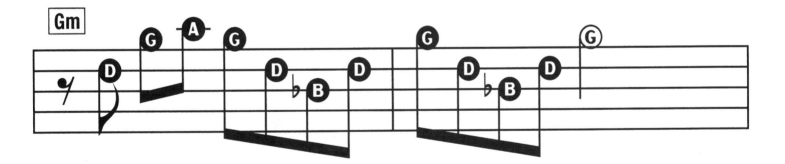

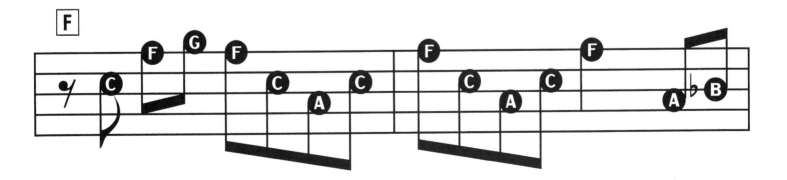

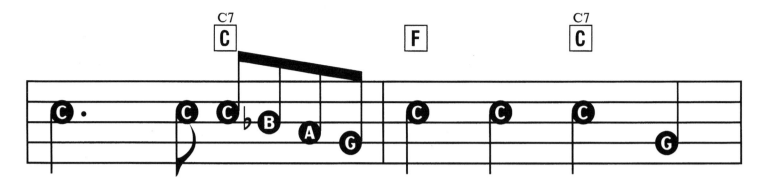

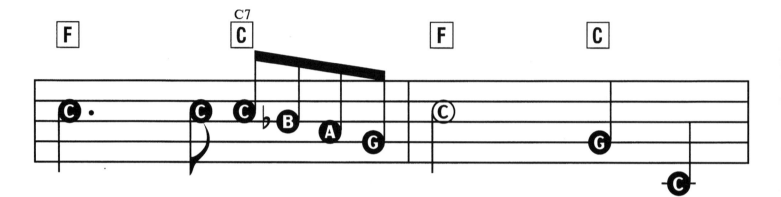

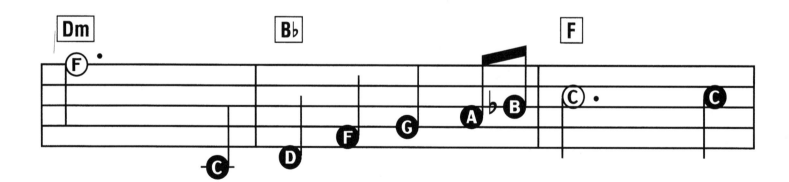

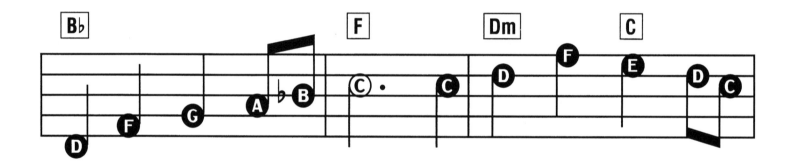

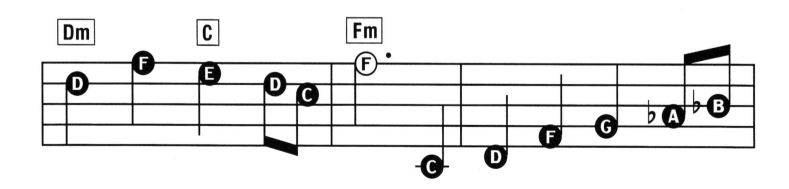

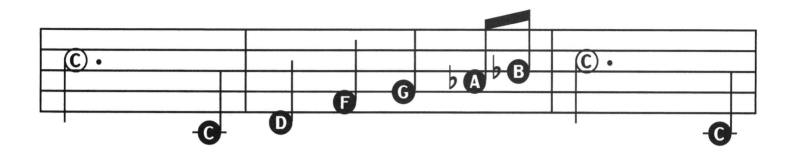

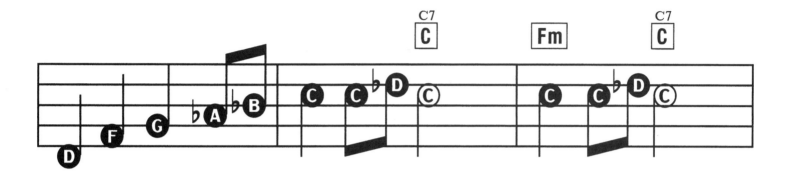

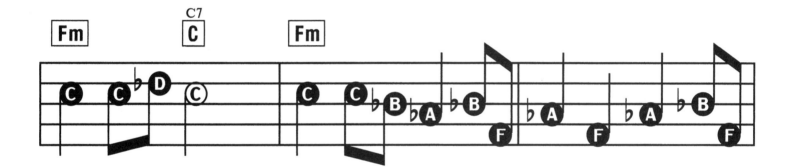

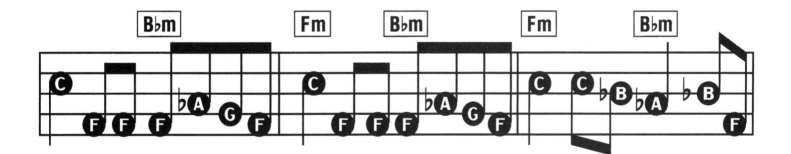

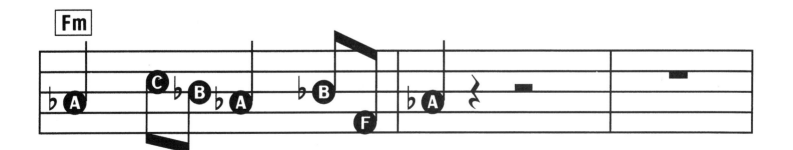

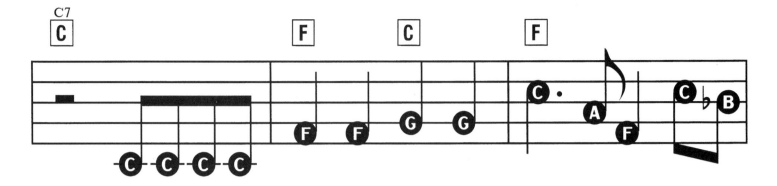

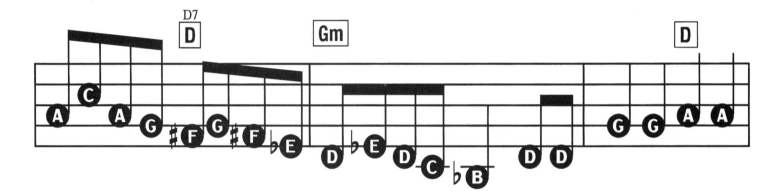

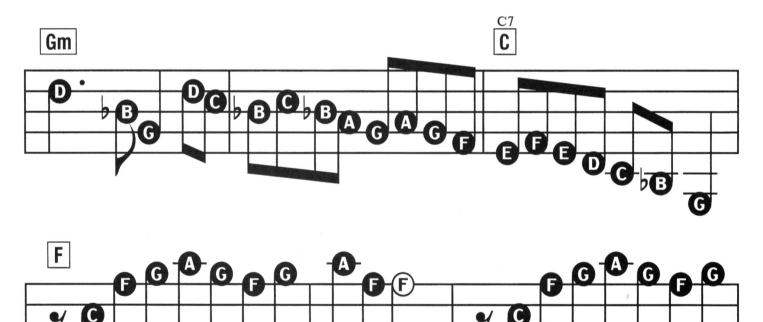

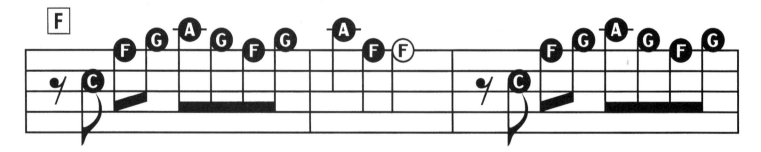

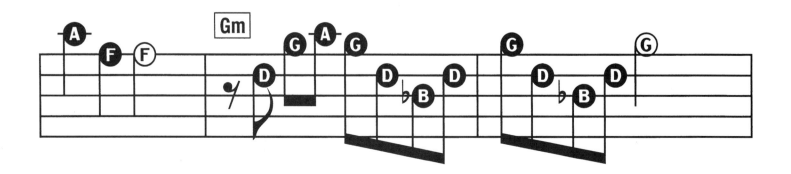

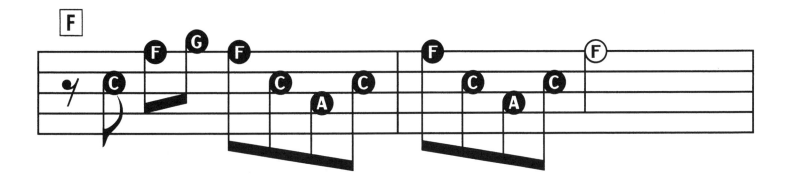

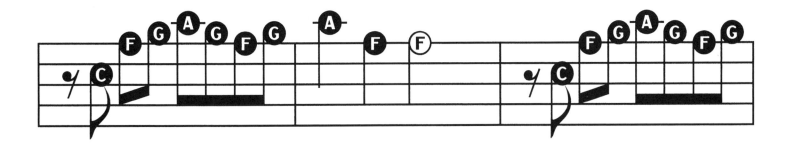

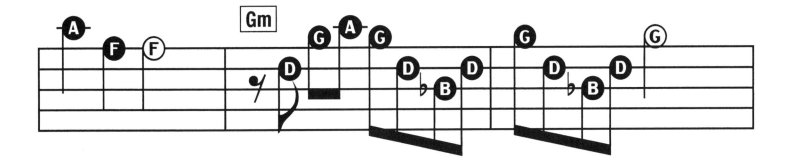

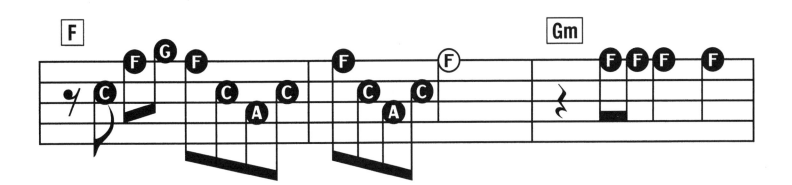

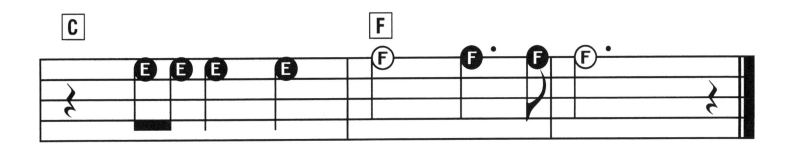

Can Can
from ORPHEUS IN THE UNDERWORLD

Registration 5
Rhythm: Polka or March

By Jacques Offenbach

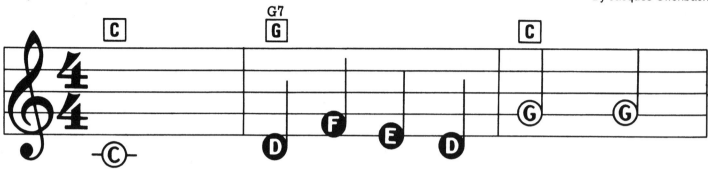

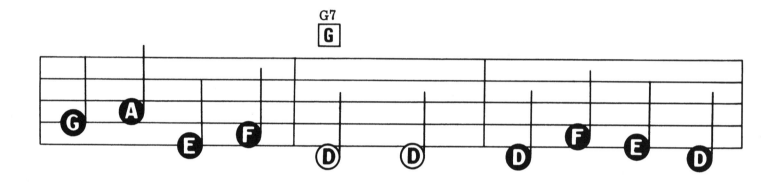

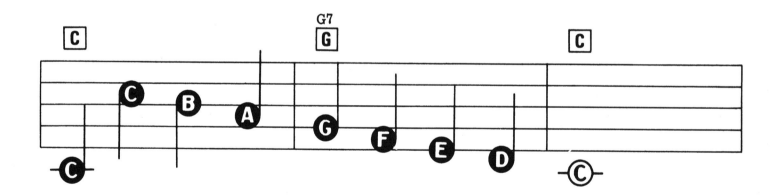

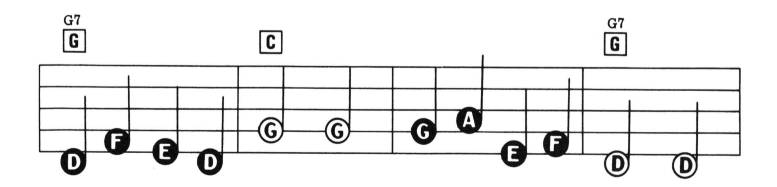

35

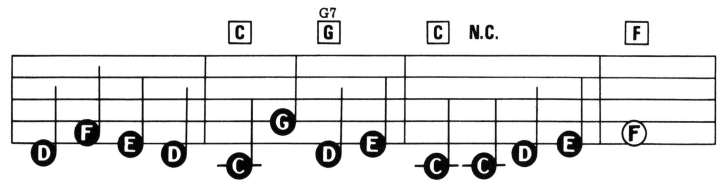

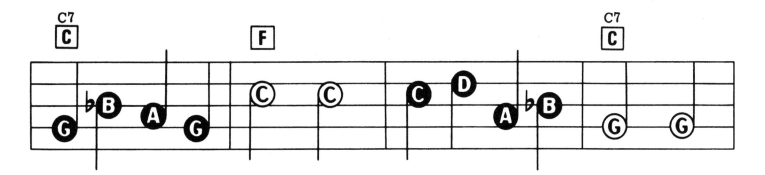

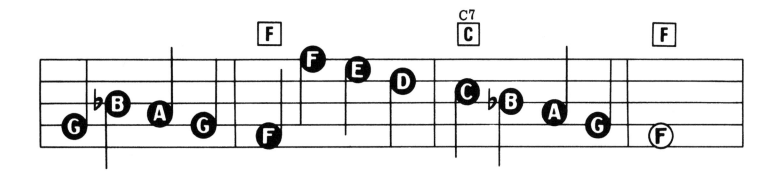

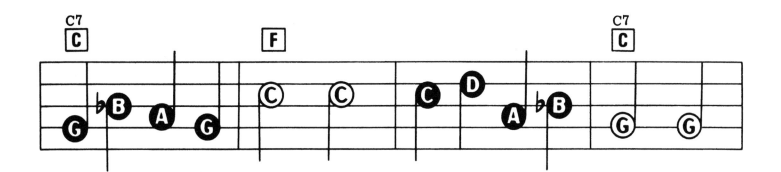

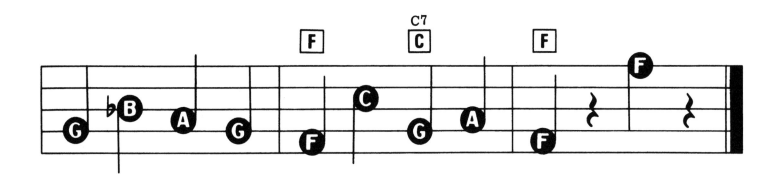

Capriccio Italien

Registration 5
Rhythm: None

By Pyotr Il'yich Tchaikovsky

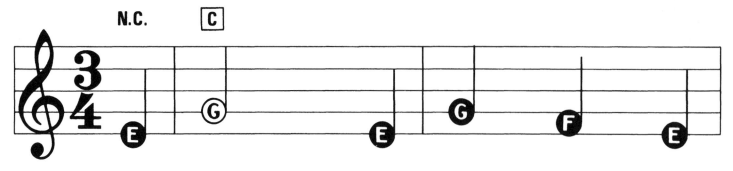

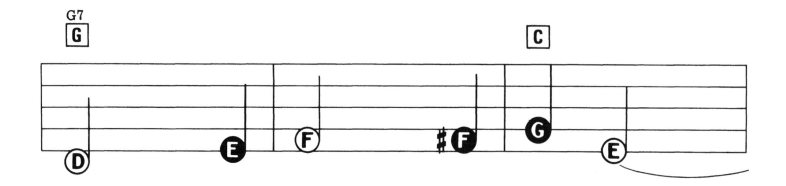

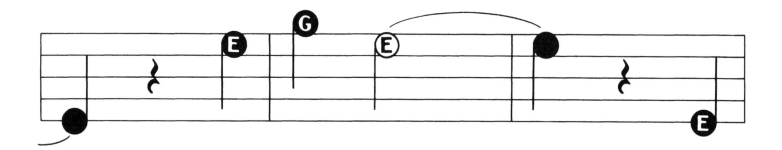

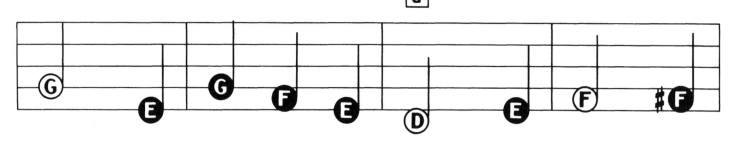

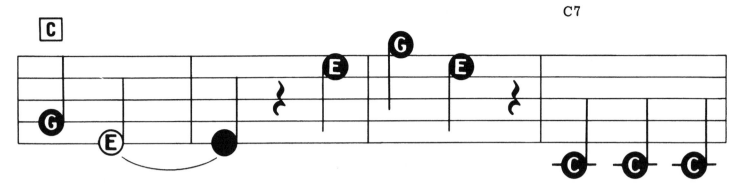

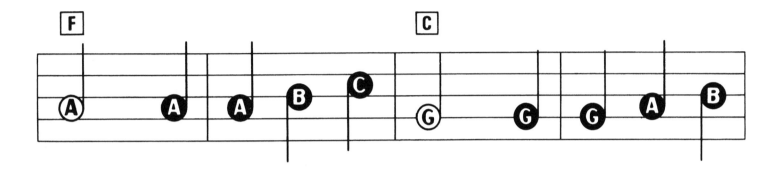

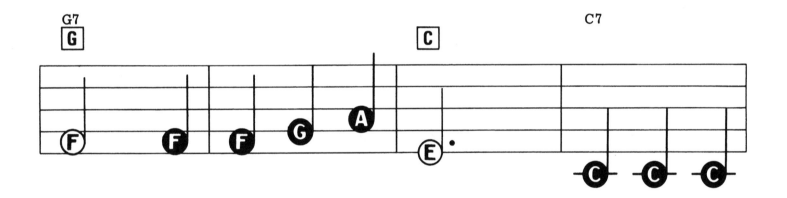

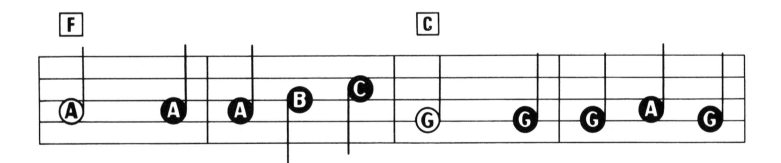

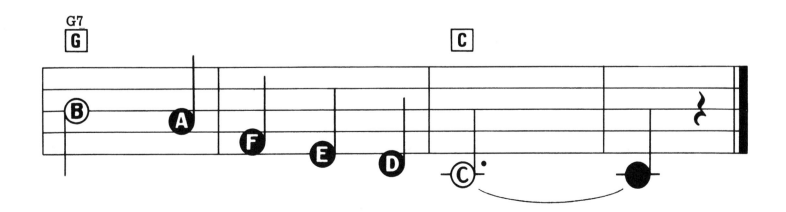

Clair de lune

Registration 8
Rhythm: None

By Claude Debussy

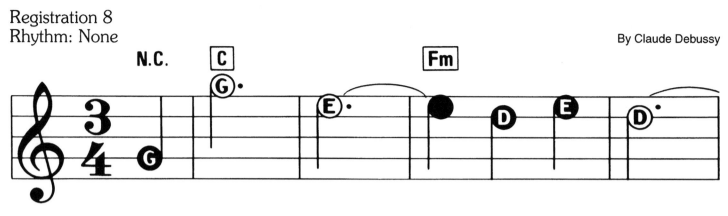

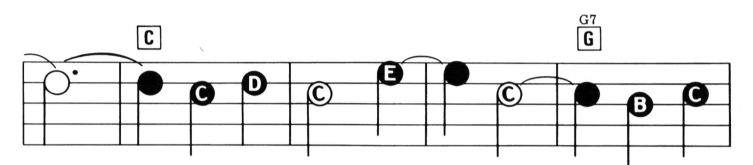

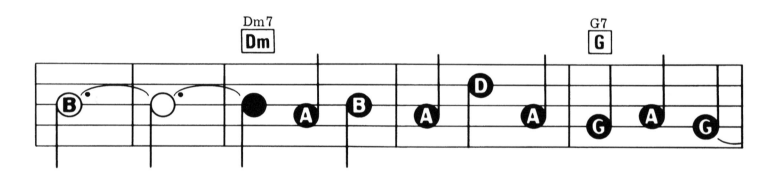

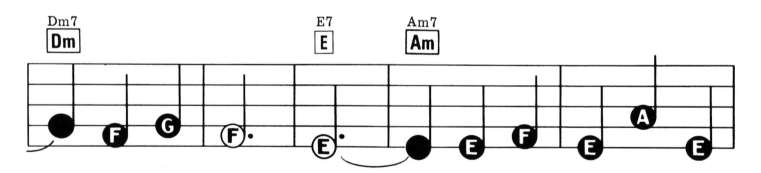

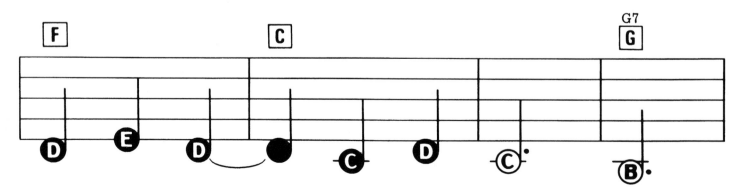

39

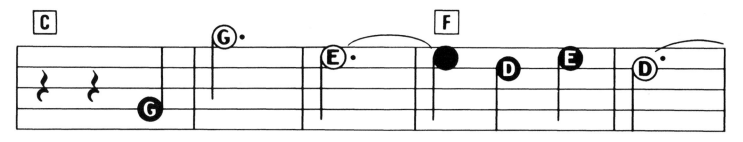

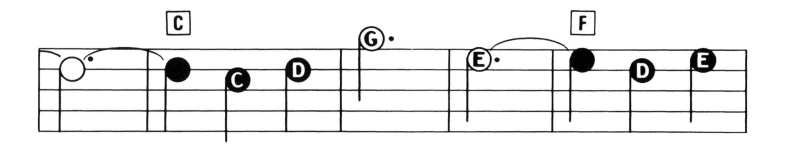

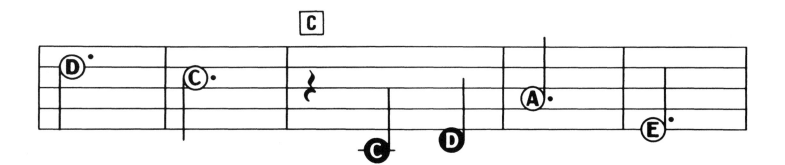

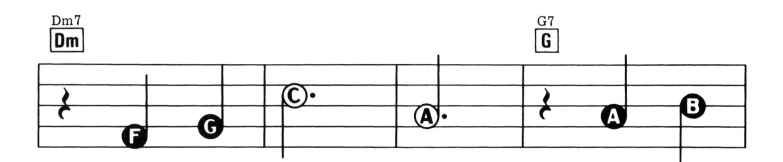

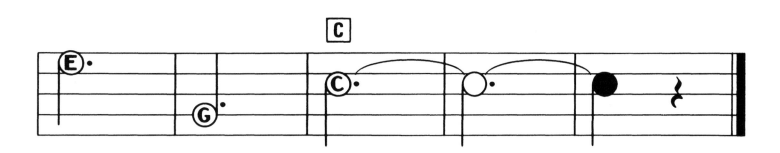

Dance of the Sugar Plum Fairy

from THE NUTCRACKER

Registration 7
Rhythm: March or None

By Pyotr Il'yich Tchaikovsky

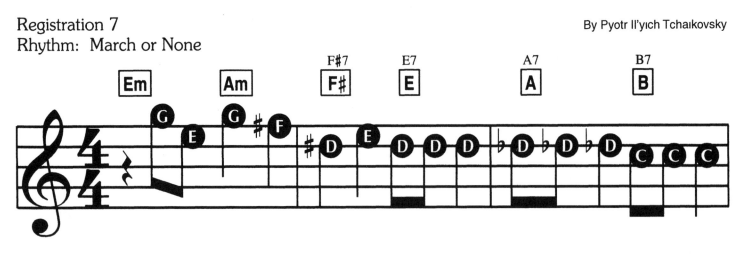

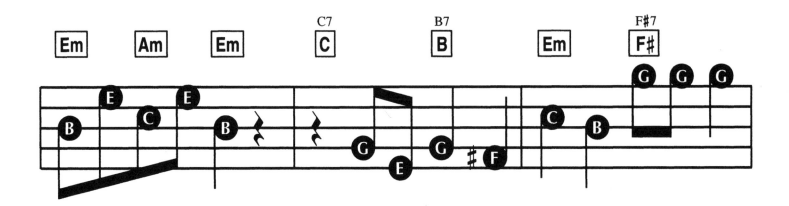

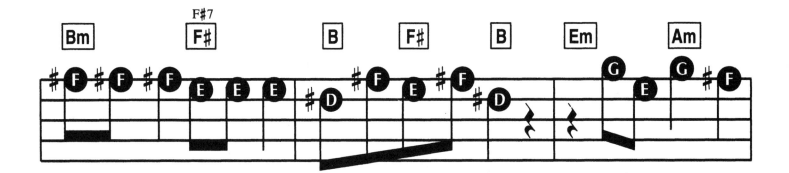

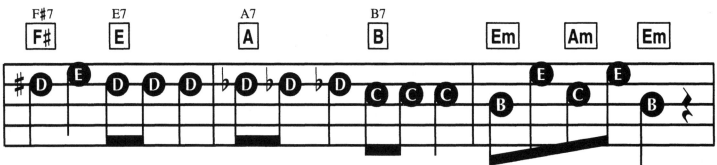

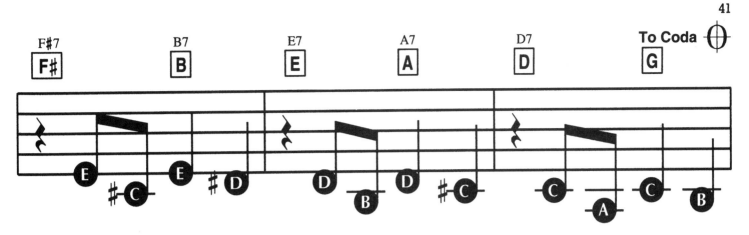

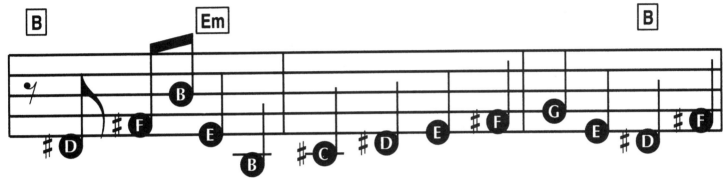

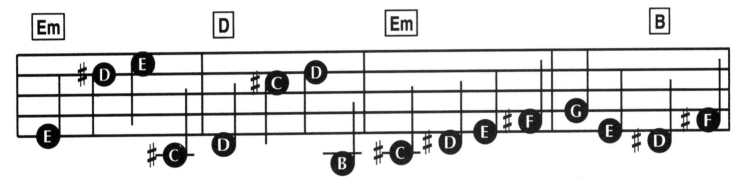

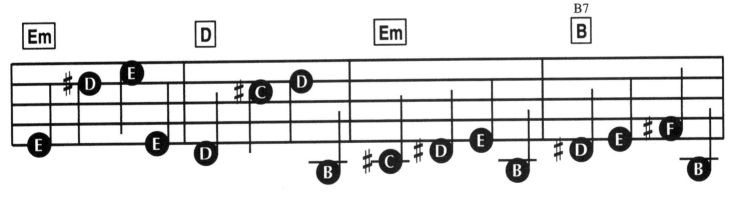

D.C. al Coda
(Return to beginning
Play to ⊕ and
Skip to Coda)

CODA ⊕

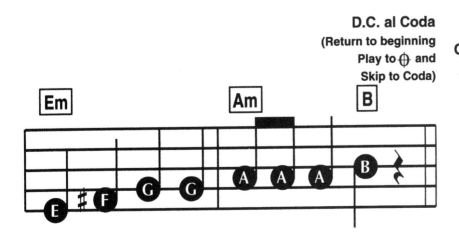

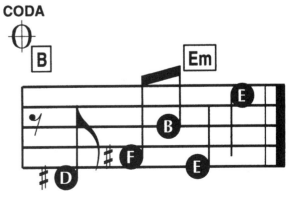

Emperor Waltz

Registration 3
Rhythm: Waltz

By Johann Strauss, Jr

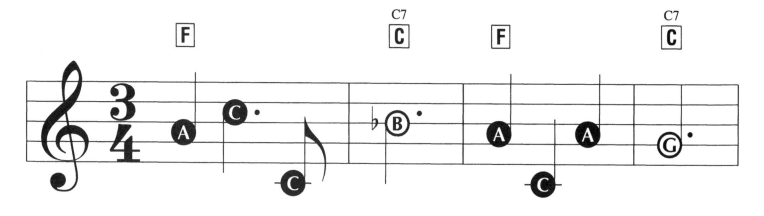

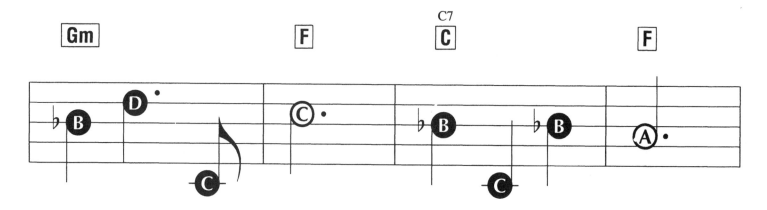

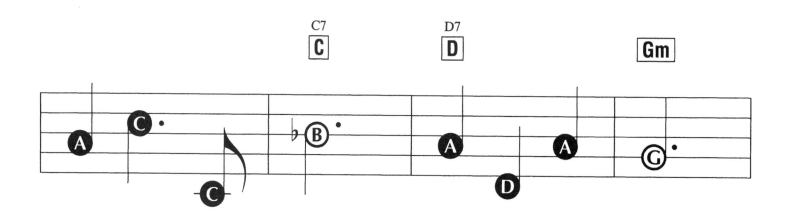

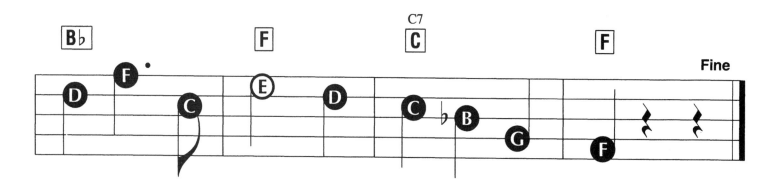

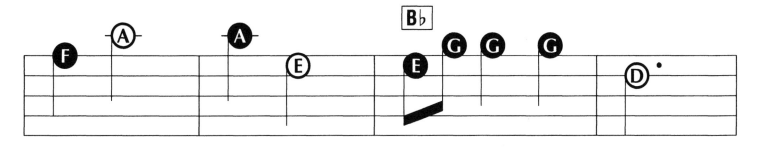

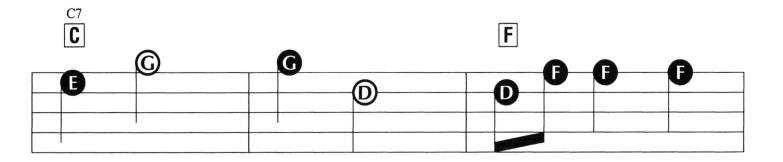

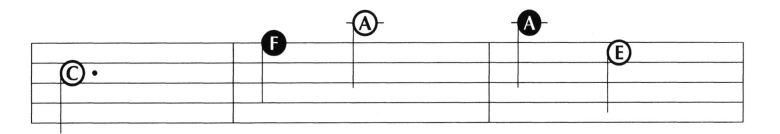

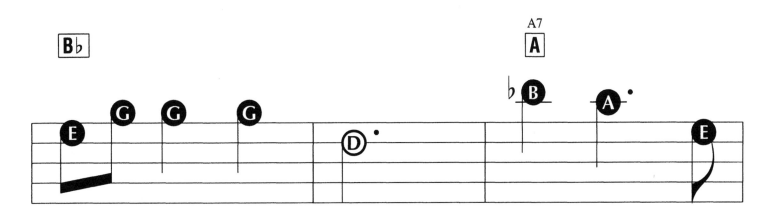

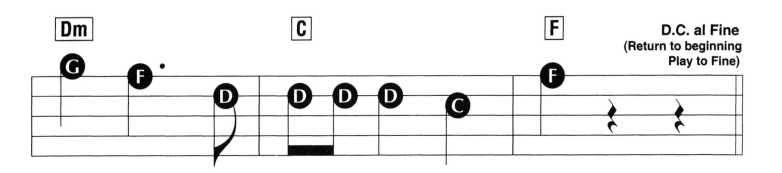

D.C. al Fine
(Return to beginning
Play to Fine)

Für Elise

Registration 6
Rhythm: None

By Ludwig van Beethoven

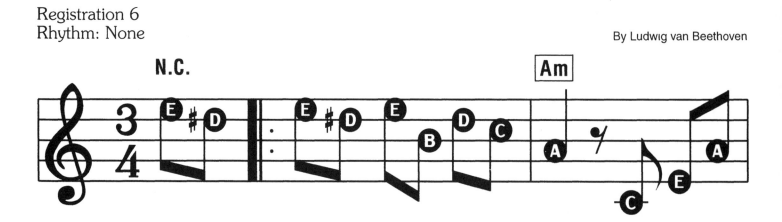

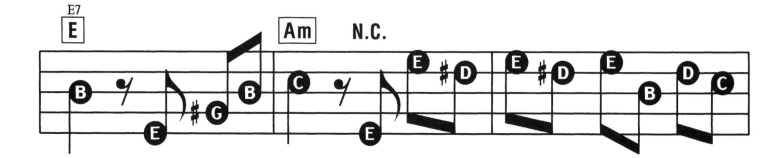

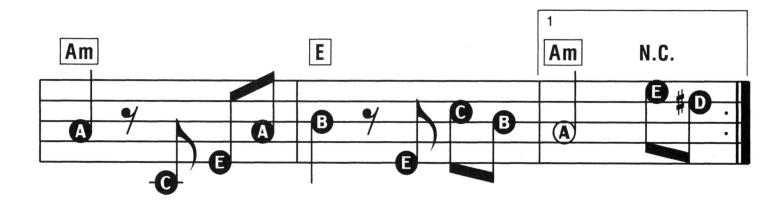

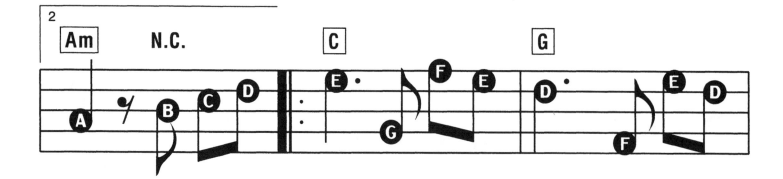

45

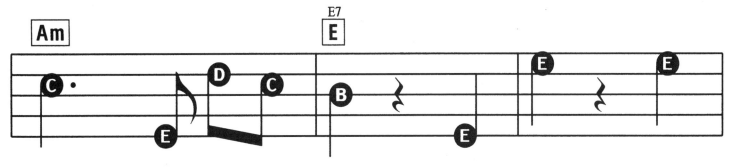

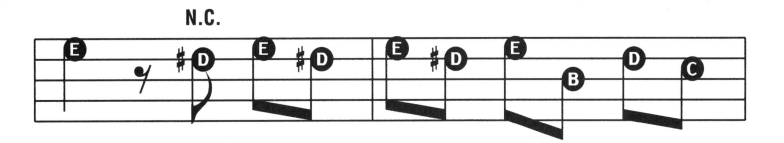

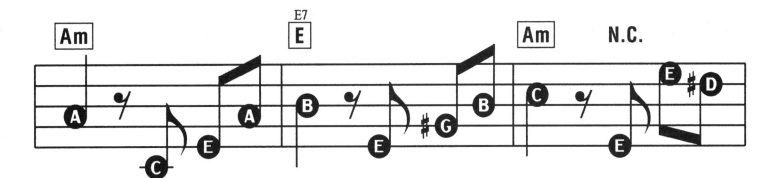

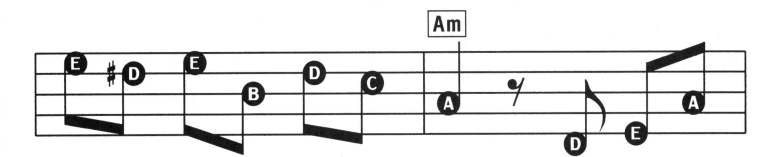

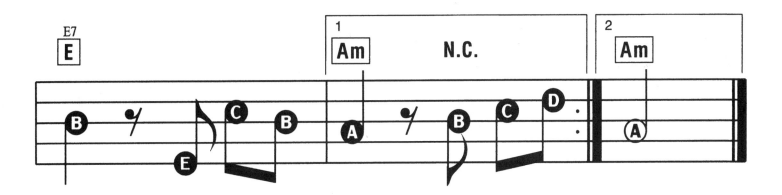

Hallelujah!
from MESSIAH

Registration 4
Rhythm: March

By George Frideric Handel

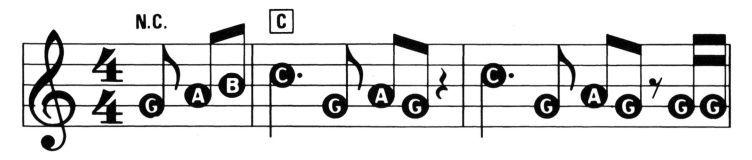

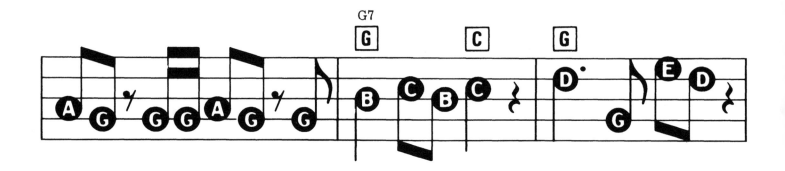

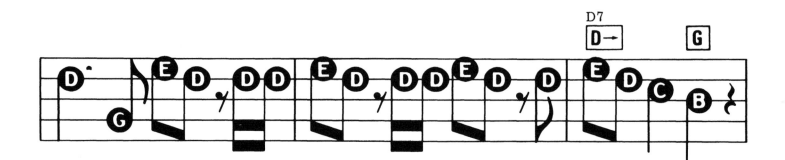

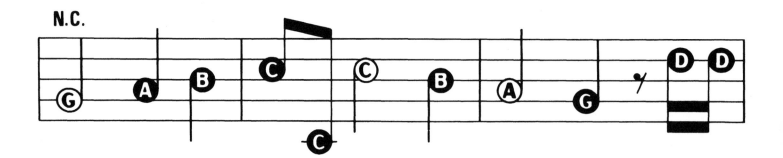

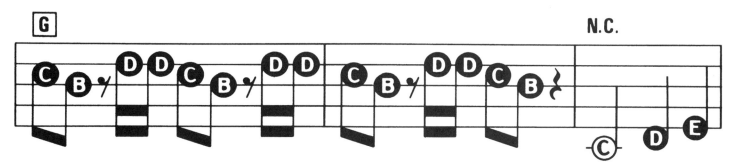

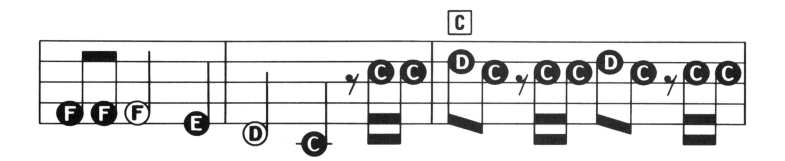

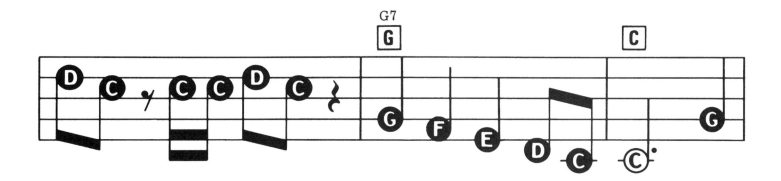

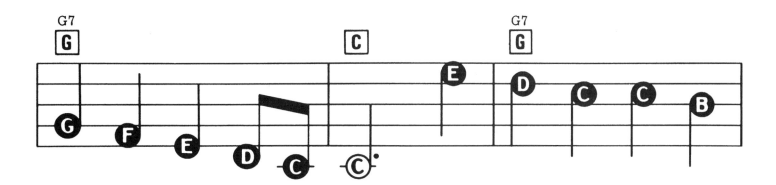

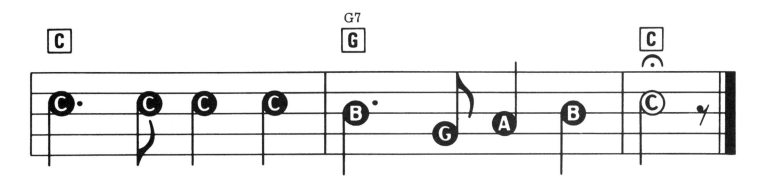

In the Hall of the Mountain King
from PEER GYNT

Registration 4
Rhythm: Fox Trot

By Edvard Grieg

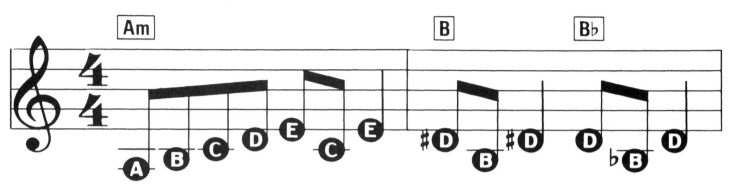

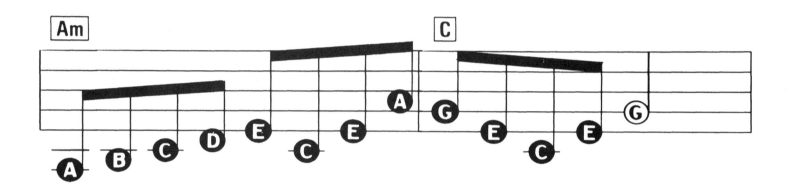

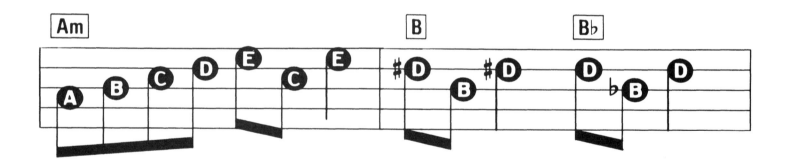

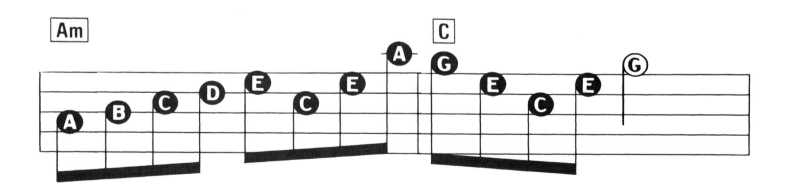

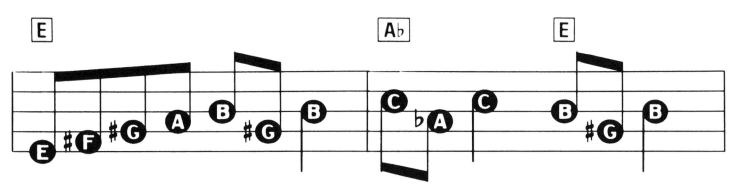

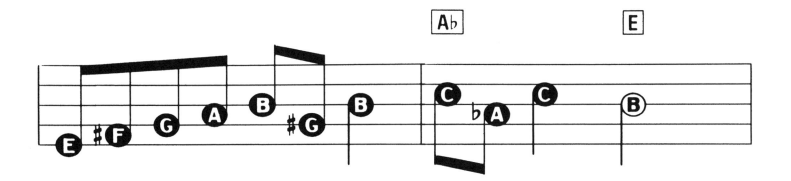

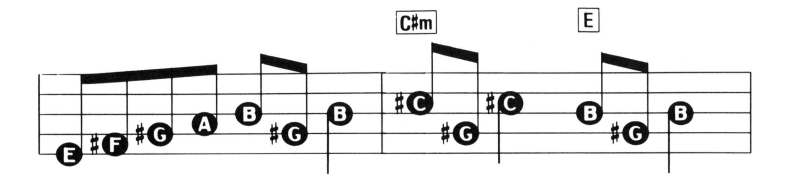

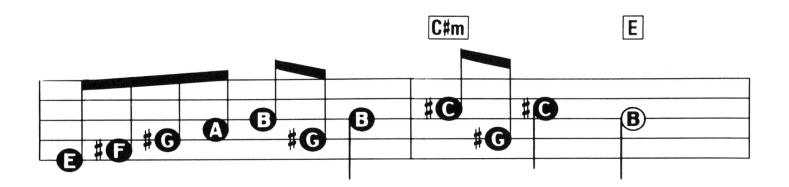

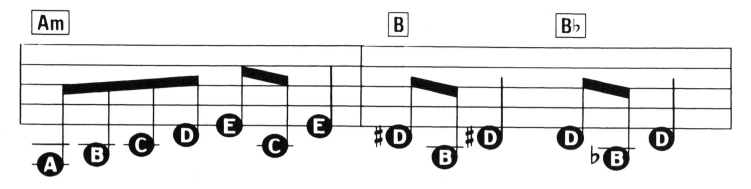

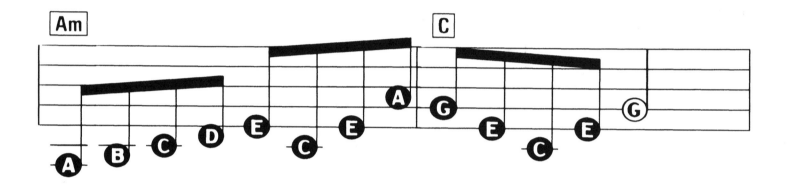

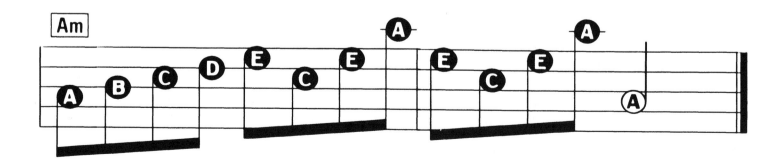

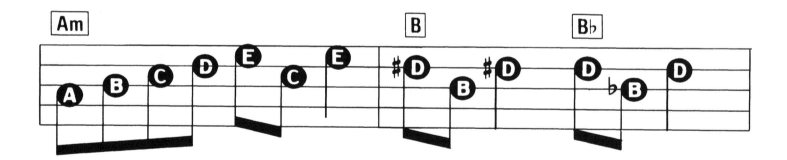

Libiamo
from LA TRAVIATA (THE FALLEN WOMAN)

Registration 4
Rhythm: Waltz

By Giuseppe Verdi

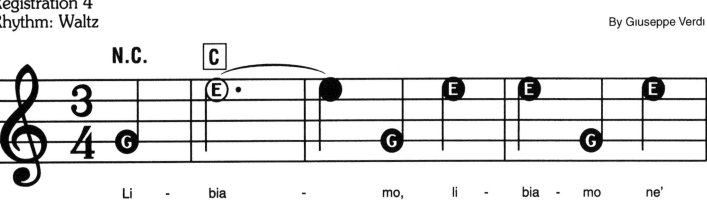

Li - bia - mo, li - bia - mo ne'

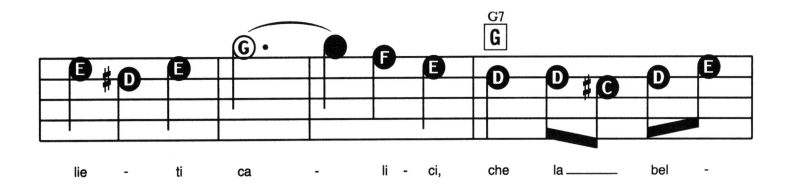

lie - ti ca - li - ci, che la _____ bel -

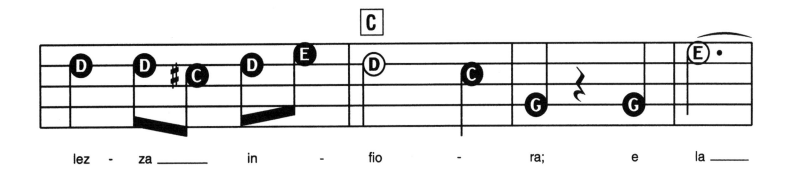

lez - za _____ in - fio - ra; e la _____

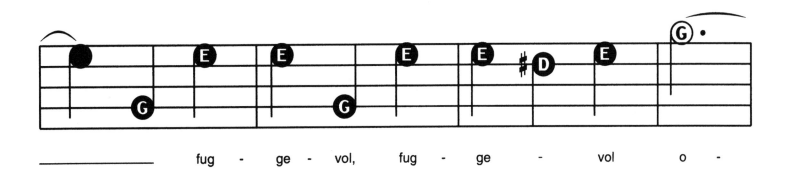

_____ fug - ge - vol, fug - ge - vol o -

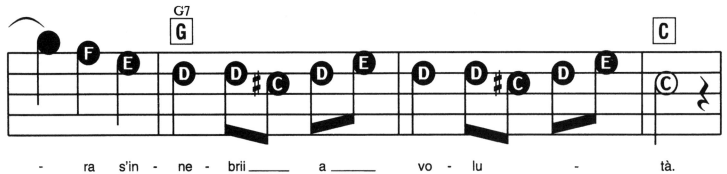

- ra s'in - ne - brii____ a ____ vo - lu - tà.

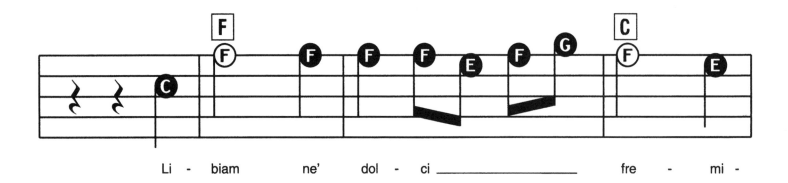

Li - biam ne' dol - ci _____ fre - mi -

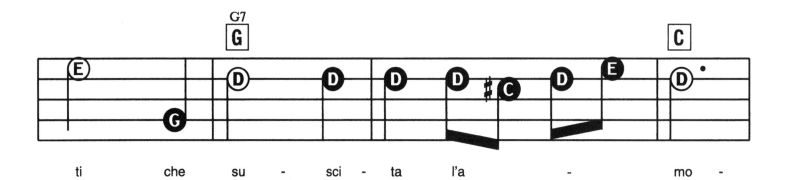

ti che su - sci - ta l'a - mo -

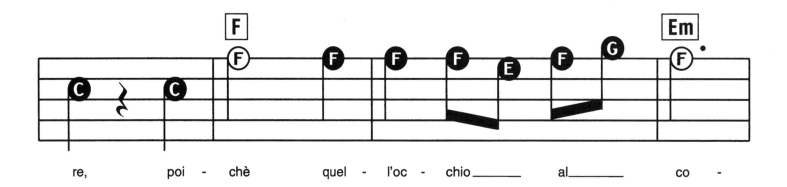

re, poi - chè quel - l'oc - chio____ al____ co -

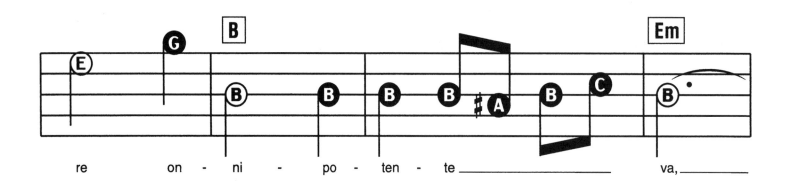

re on - ni - po - ten - te _____ va,____

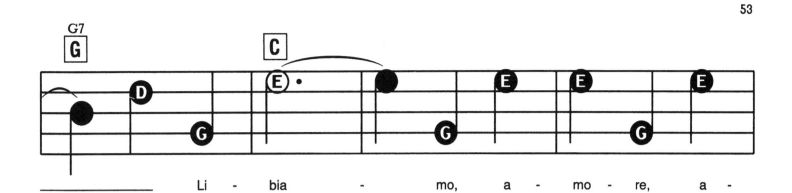

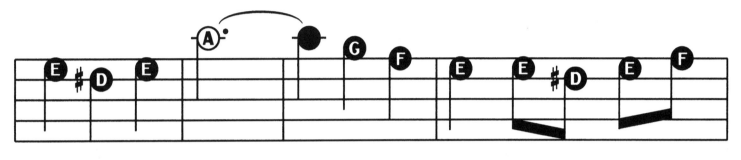

Li - bia - mo, a - mo - re, a -

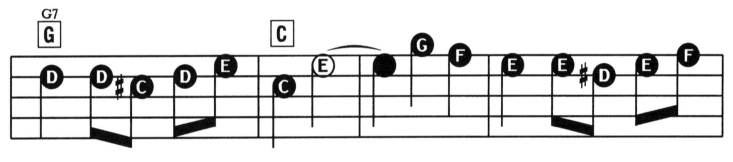

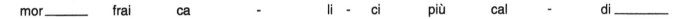

mor _____ frai ca - li - ci più cal - di _____

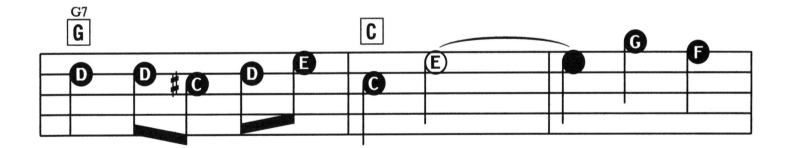

ba - ci _____ a - vra.

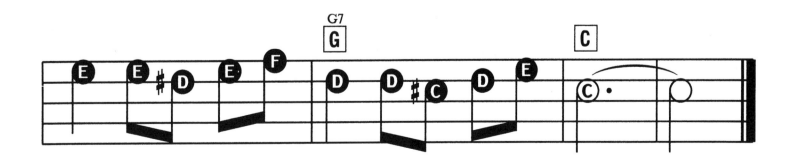

Jesu, Joy of Man's Desiring

Registration 2
Rhythm: None

By Johann Sebastian Bach

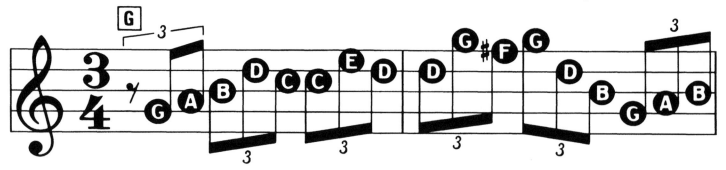

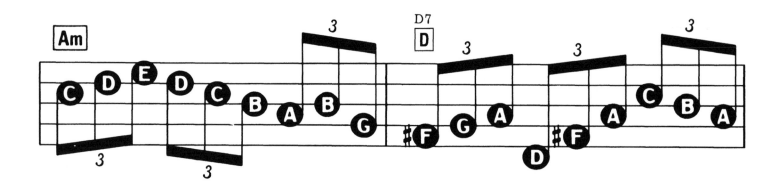

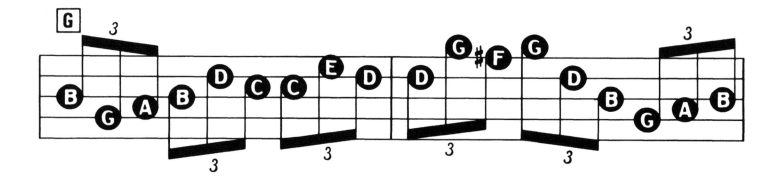

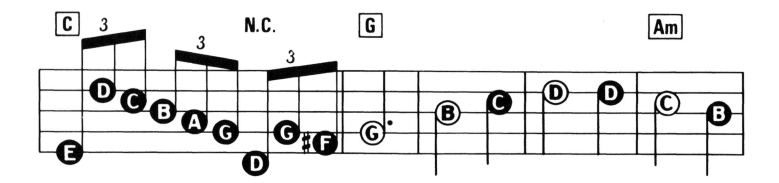

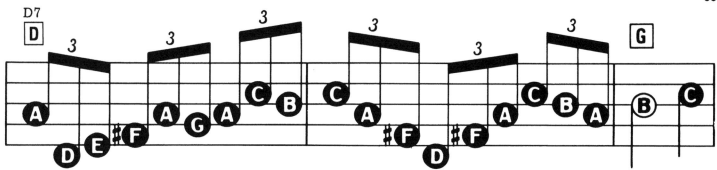

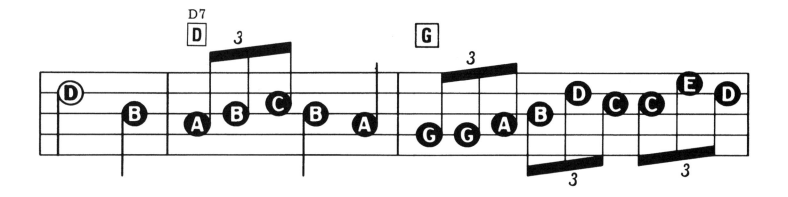

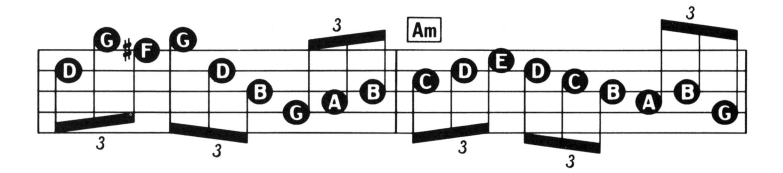

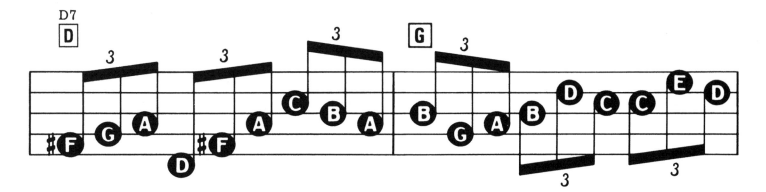

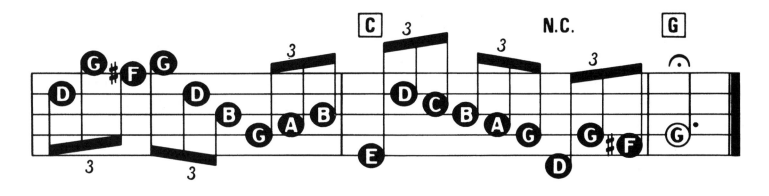

La donna è mobile
from RIGOLETTO

Registration 4
Rhythm: Waltz

By Giuseppe Verdi

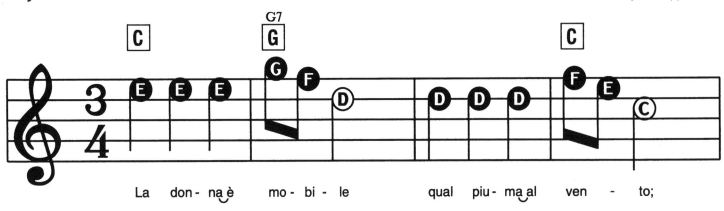

La don - na è mo - bi - le qual piu - ma al ven - to;

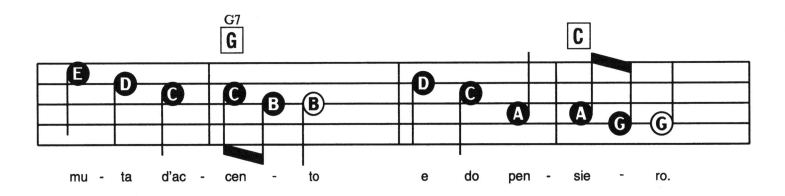

mu - ta d'ac - cen - to e do pen - sie - ro.

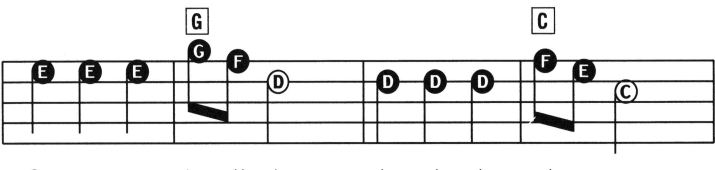

Sem - pre un a - ma - bi - le leg - gia - dro vi - so,

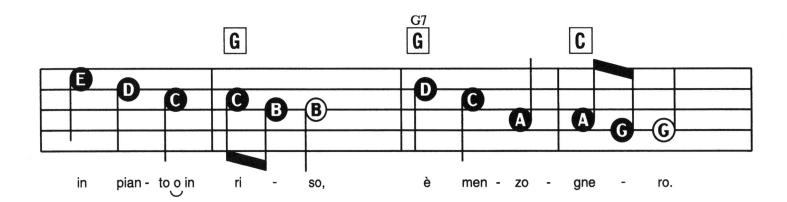

in pian - to o in ri - so, è men - zo - gne - ro.

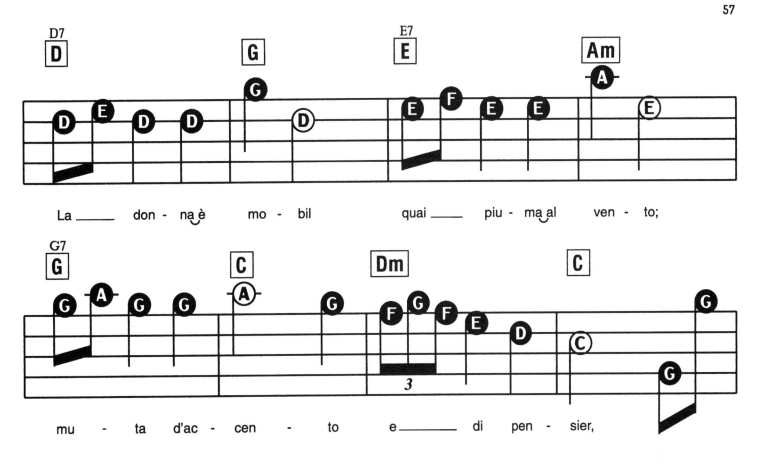

La _____ don - na‿è mo - bil quai _____ piu - ma‿al ven - to;

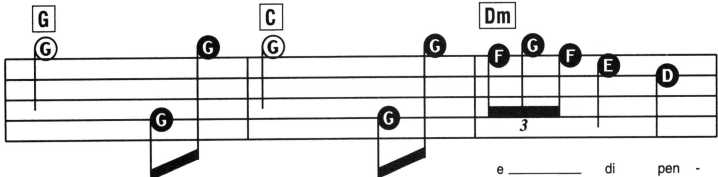

mu - ta d'ac - cen - to e _____ di pen - sier,

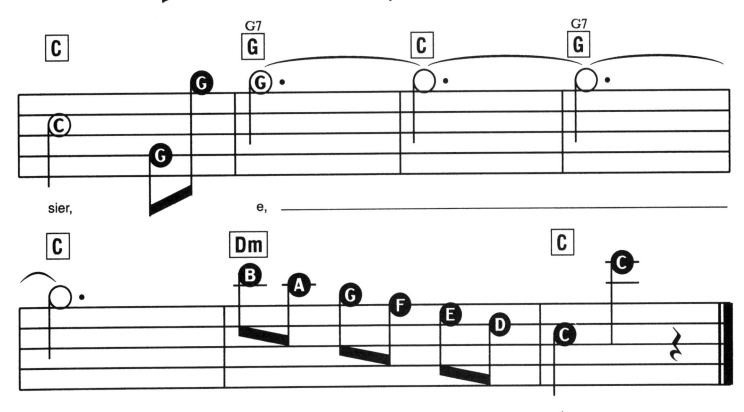

e _____ di pen -

sier, e, _____

_____ e _____ di _____ pen - sier.

Liebestraume
(Dream of Love)

Registration 10
Rhythm: Waltz

By Franz Liszt

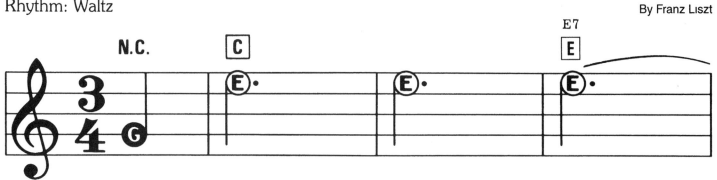

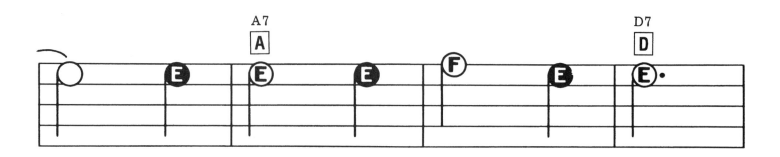

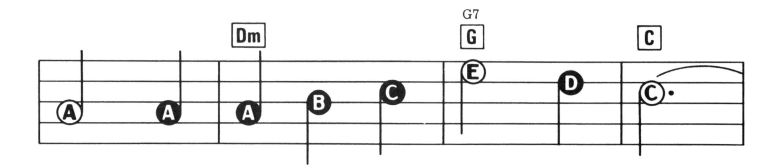

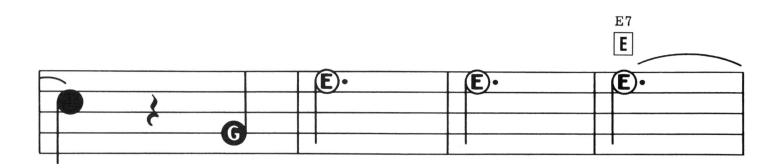

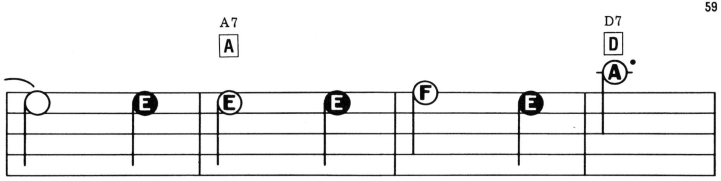

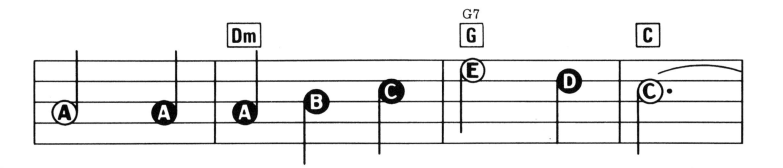

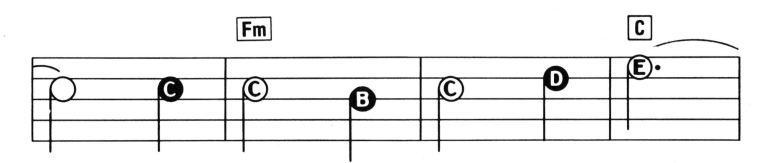

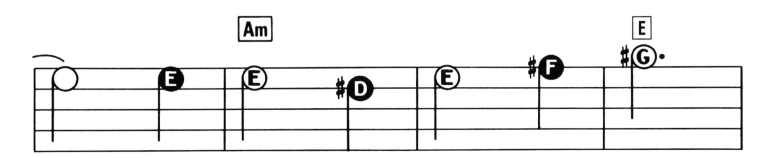

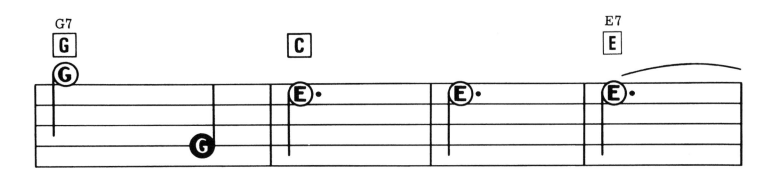

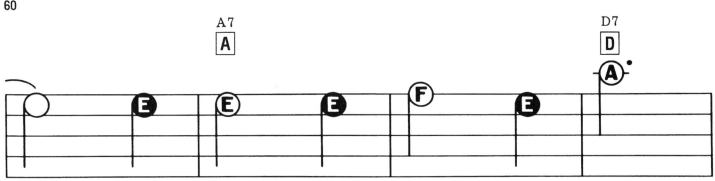

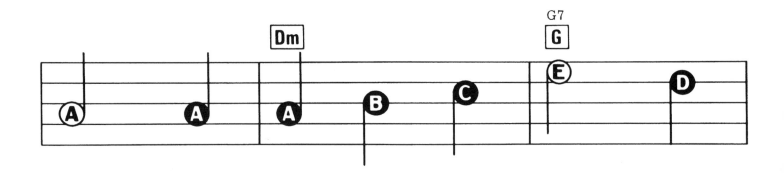

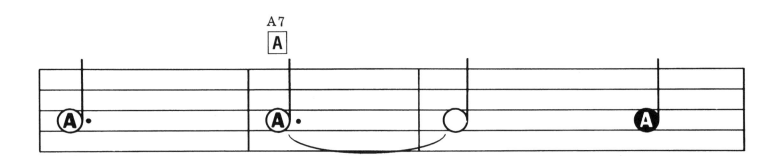

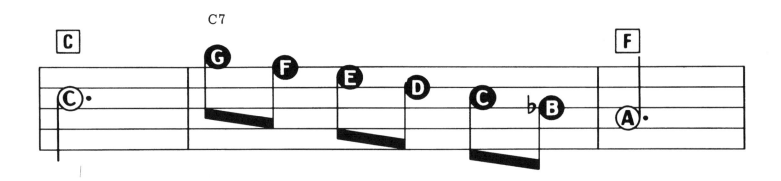

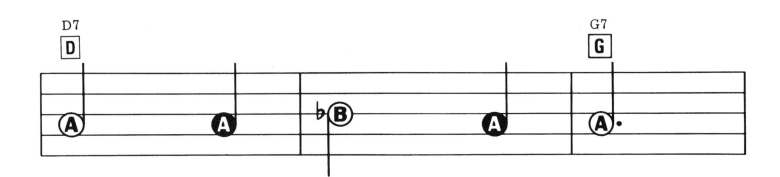

61

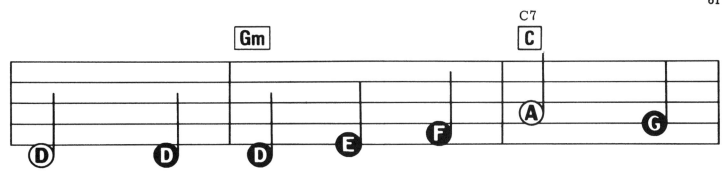

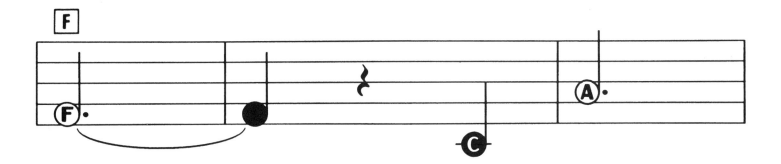

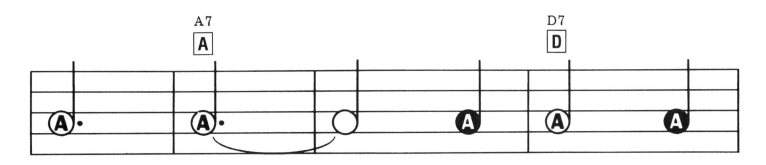

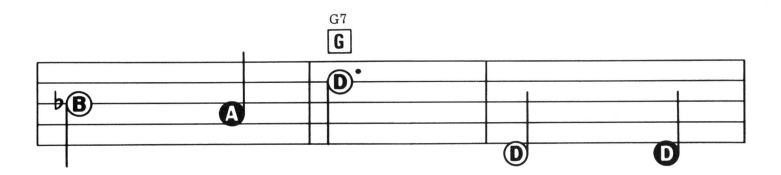

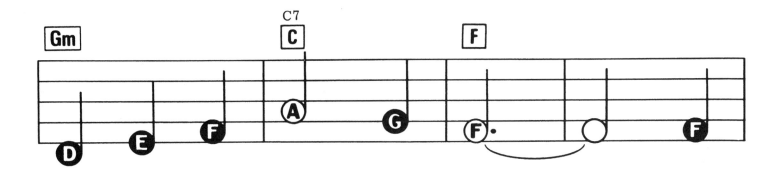

62

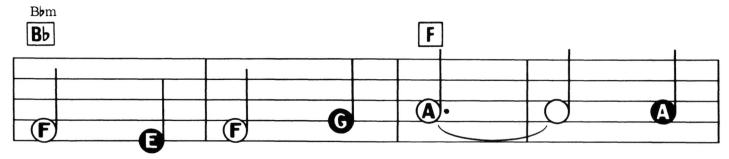

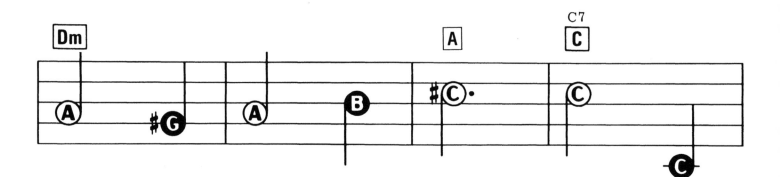

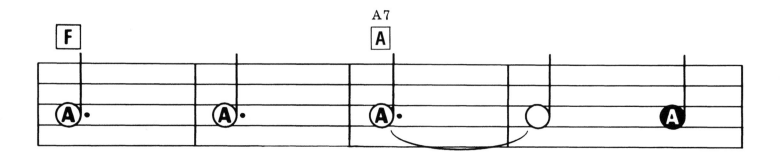

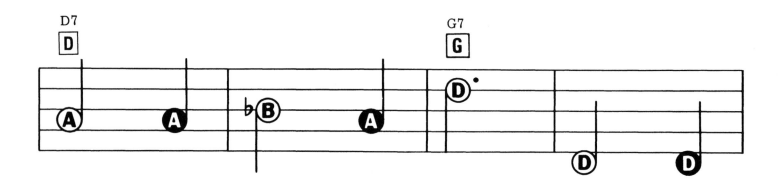

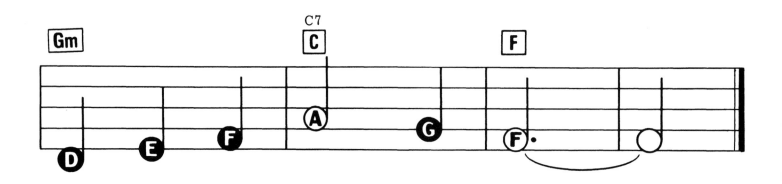

Melody in F

Registration 10
Rhythm: Ballad or Fox Trot

By Anton Rubinstein

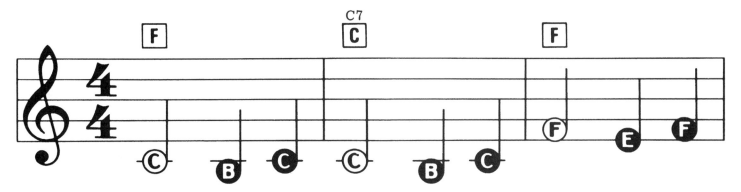

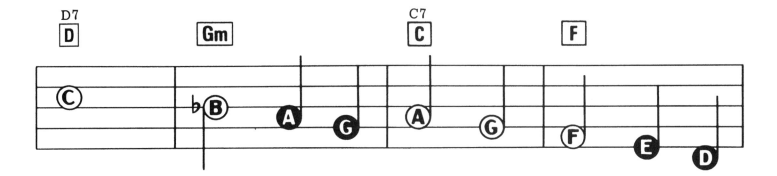

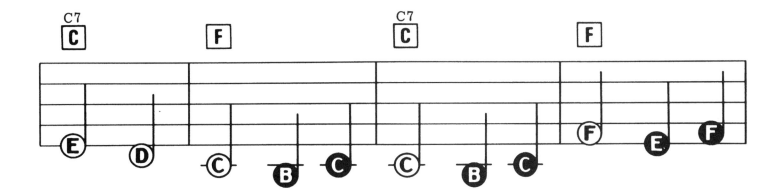

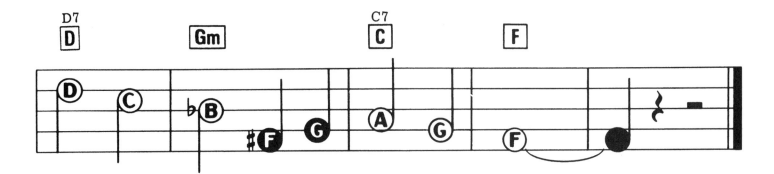

M'appari tutt' amor
from MARTHA

Registration 10
Rhythm: None

By Friedrich von Flotow

65

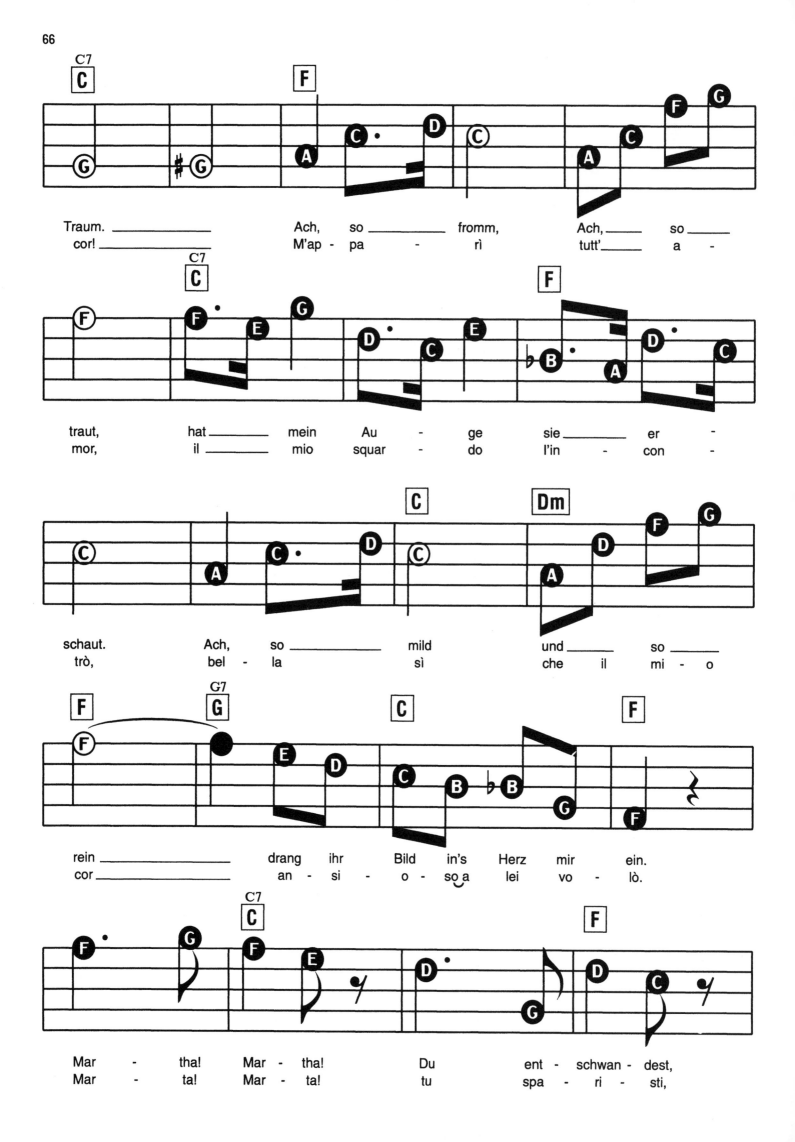

Traum. _____ Ach, so _____ fromm, Ach, _____ so _____
cor! _____ M'ap - pa - rì tutt' _____ a -

traut, hat _____ mein Au - ge sie _____ er -
mor, il _____ mio squar - do l'in - con -

schaut. Ach, so _____ mild und _____ so _____
trò, bel - la sì che il mi - o

rein _____ drang ihr Bild in's Herz mir ein.
cor _____ an - si - o - so a lei vo - lò.

Mar - tha! Mar - tha! Du ent - schwan - dest,
Mar - ta! Mar - ta! tu spa - ri - sti,

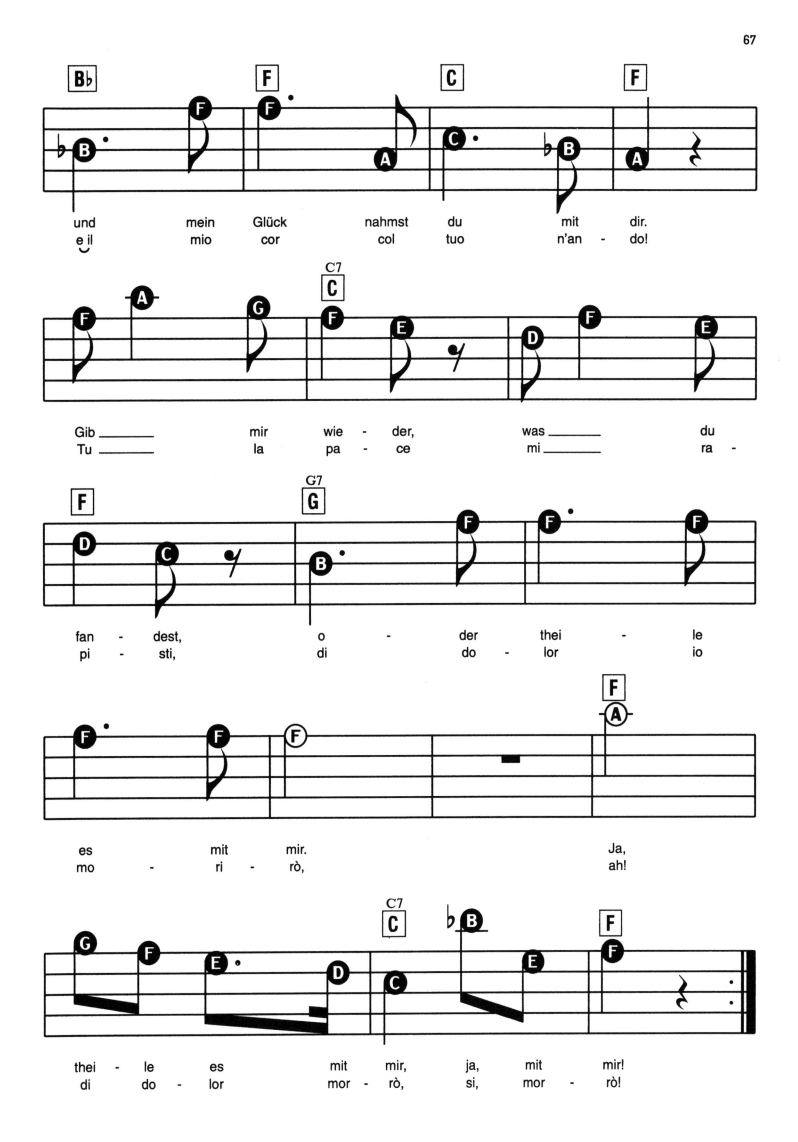

Marche Slav

Registration 5
Rhythm: March

By Pyotr Il'yich Tchaikovsky

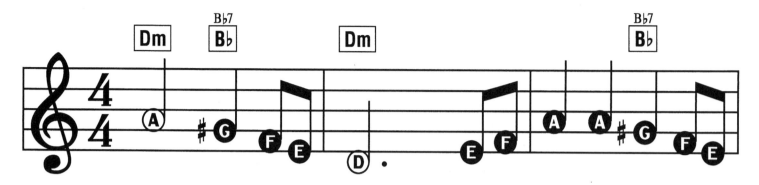

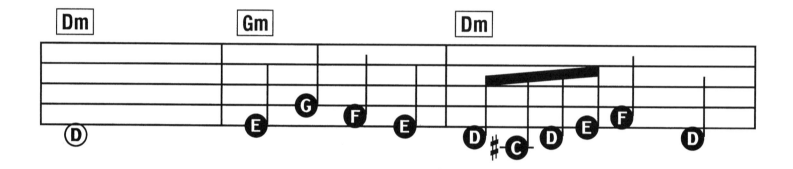

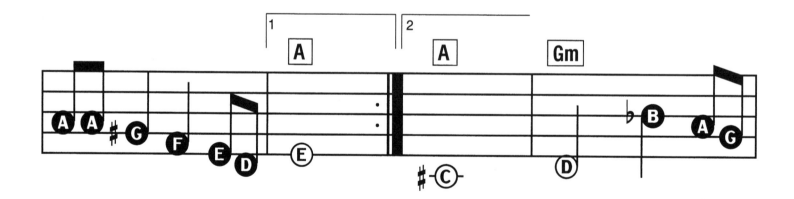

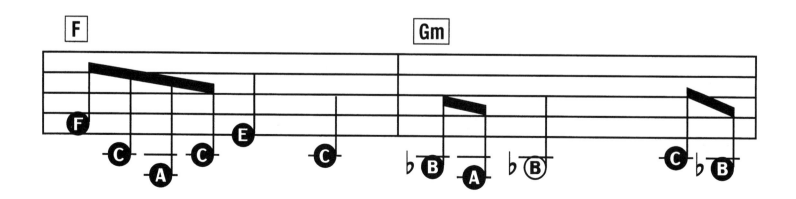

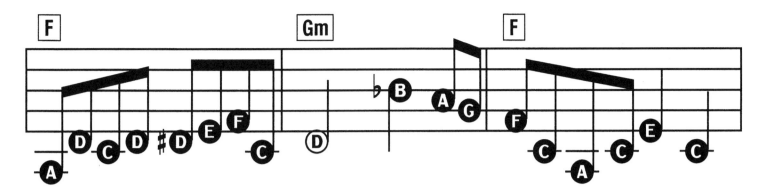

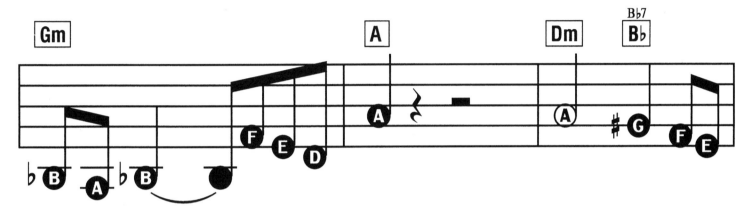

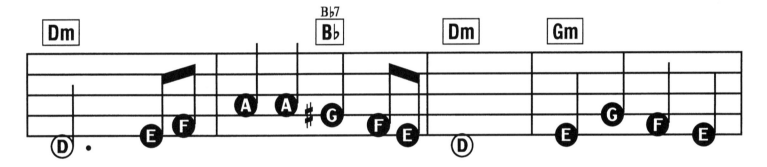

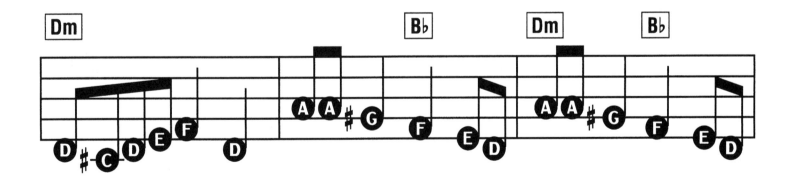

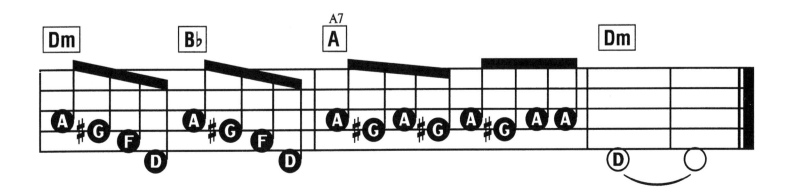

Mattinata

Registration 4
Rhythm: Waltz

By Ruggero Leoncavallo

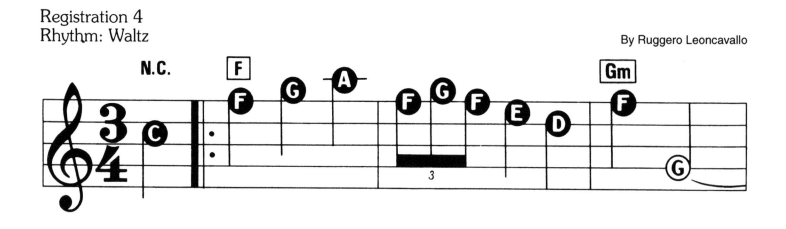

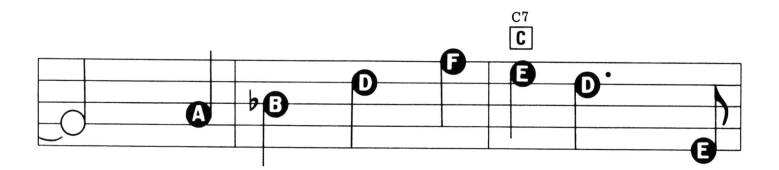

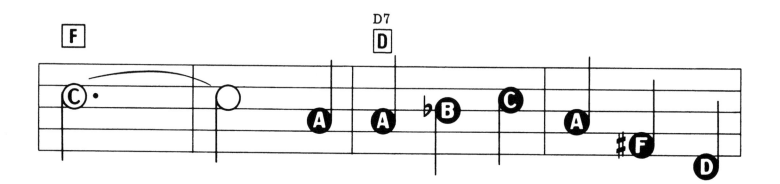

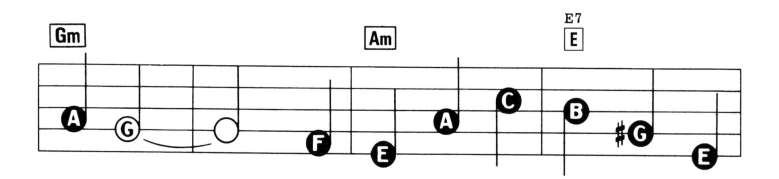

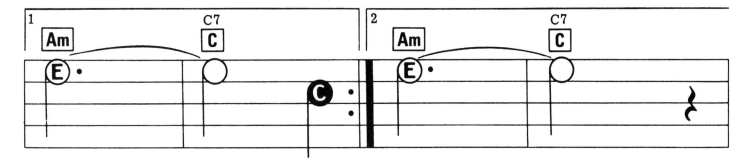
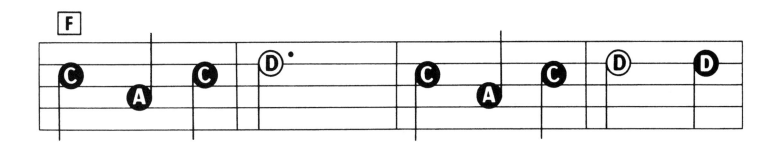
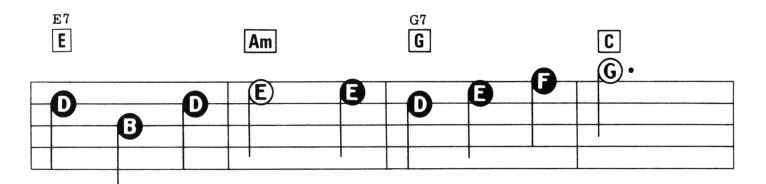
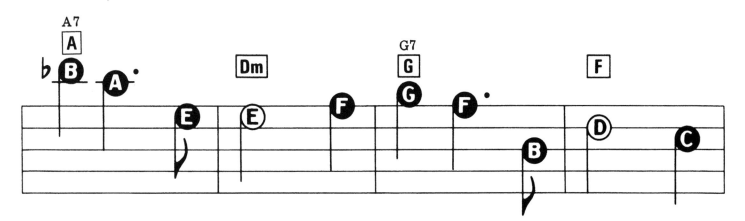
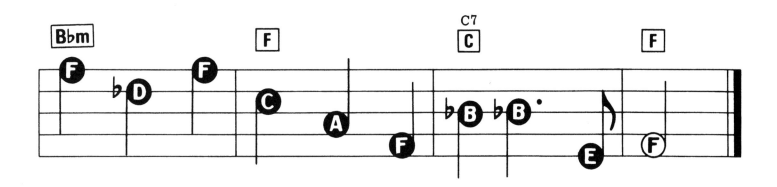

The Merry Widow Waltz

from THE MERRY WIDOW

Registration 9
Rhythm: Waltz

Words by Adrian Ross
Music by Franz Lehár

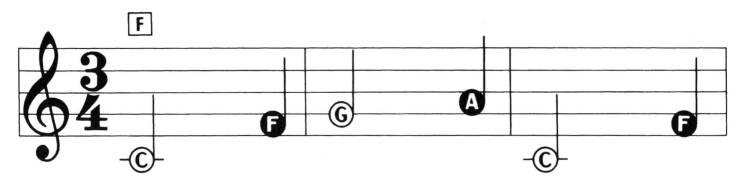

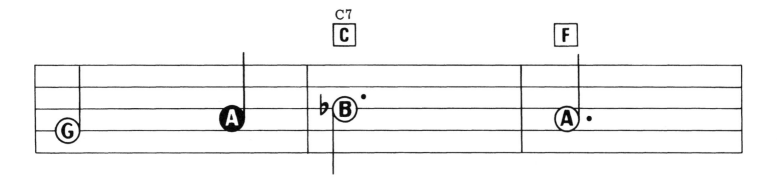

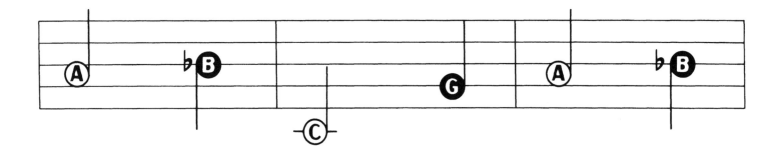

73

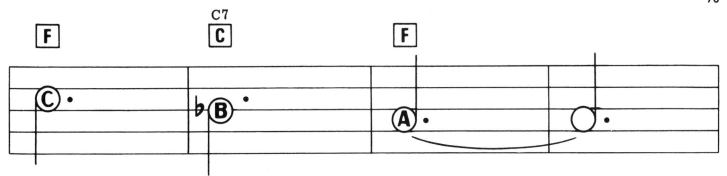
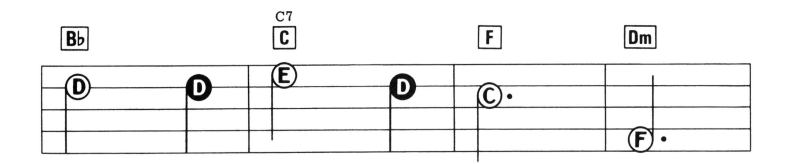
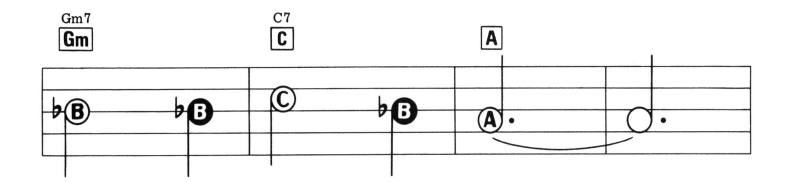
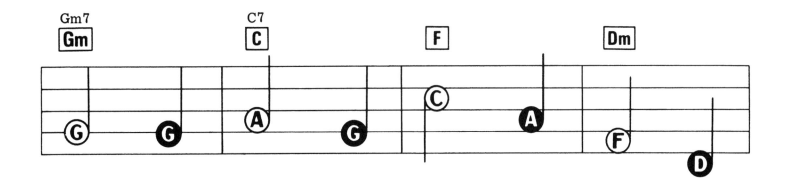
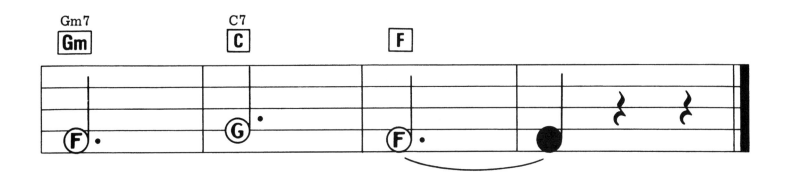

Military Polonaise

Registration 8
Rhythm: March

By Fryderyk Chopin

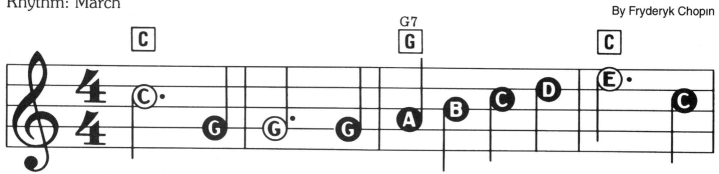

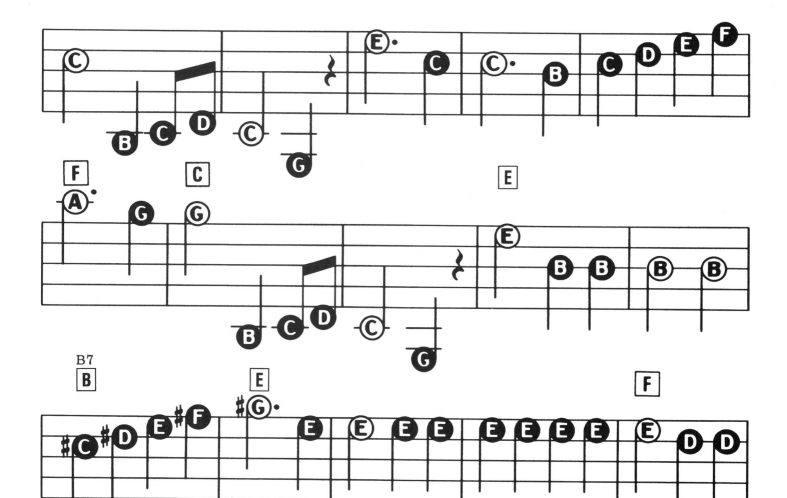

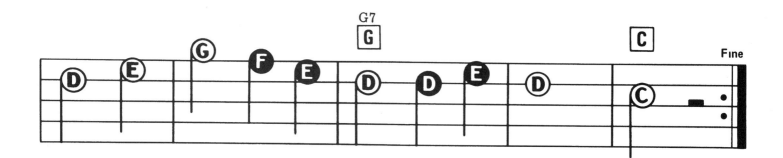

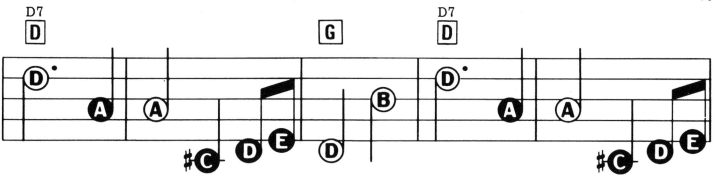

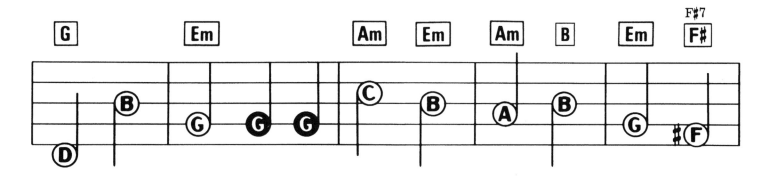

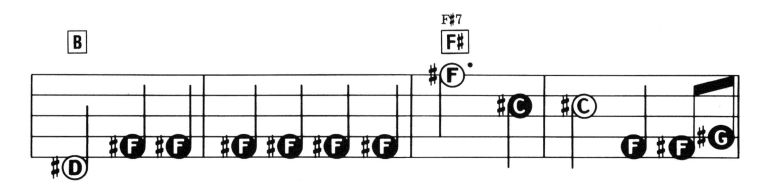

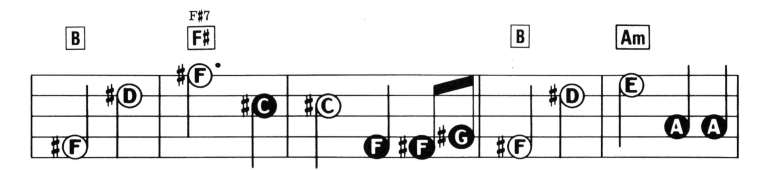

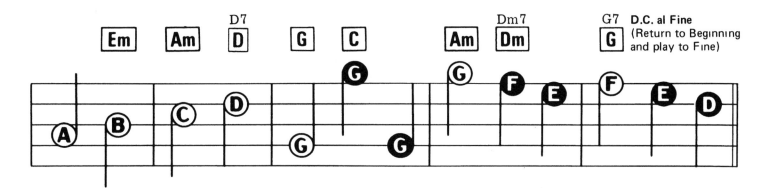

Piano Sonata No. 14 in C# Minor
"Moonlight"
Op. 27, No. 2, First Movement Theme

Registration 8
Rhythm: 8 Beat or None

By Ludwig van Beethoven

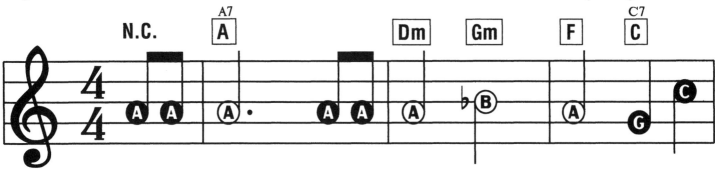

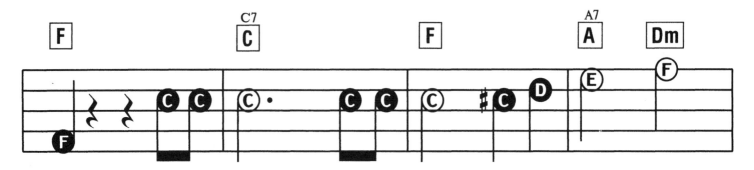

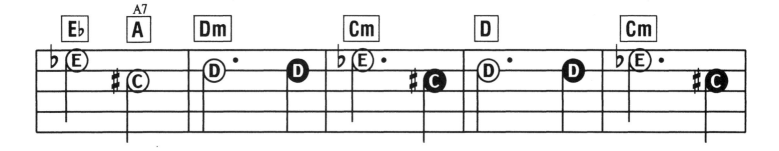

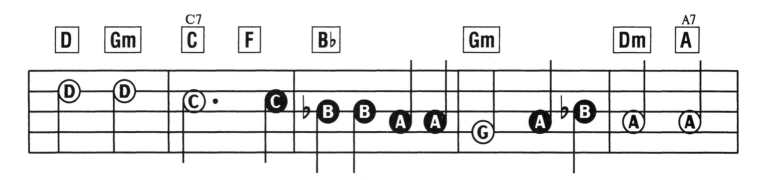

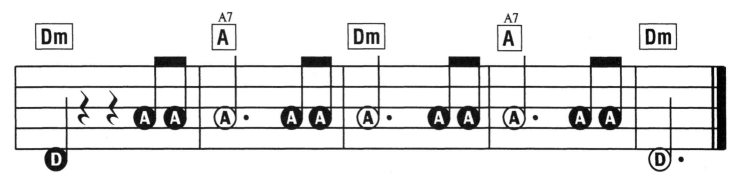

Morning
from PEER GYNT

Registration 1
Rhythm: Waltz

By Edvard Grieg

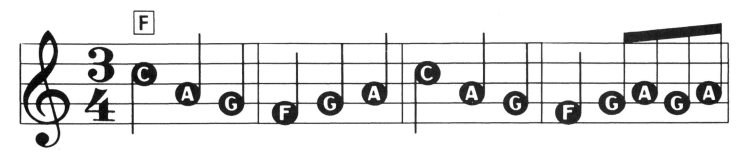

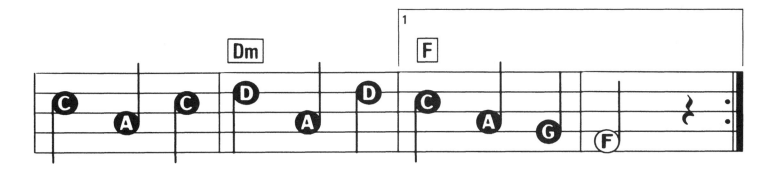

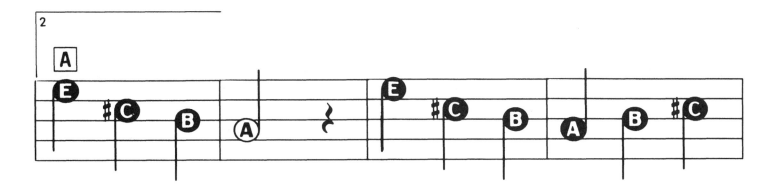

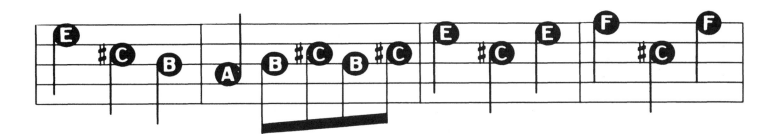

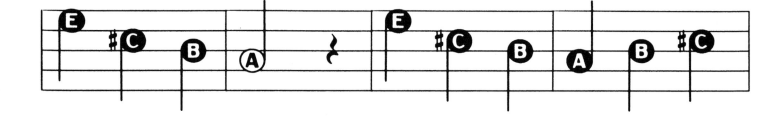

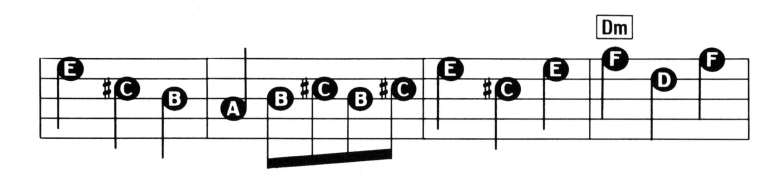

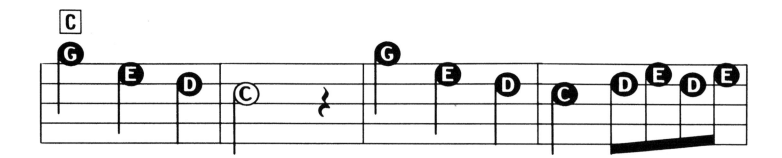

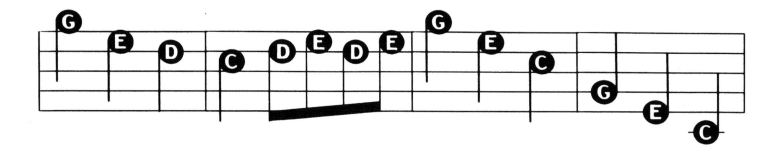

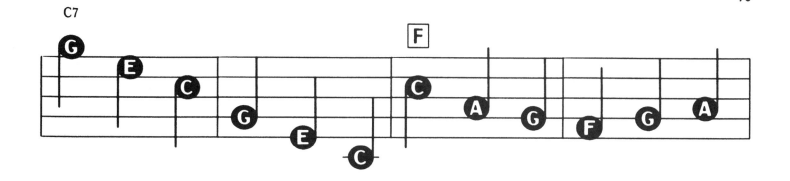
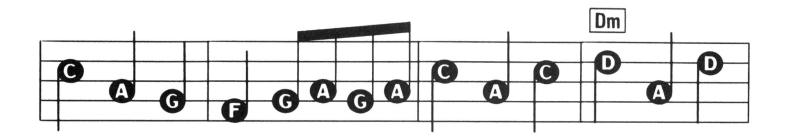
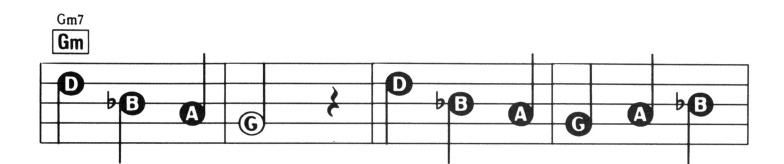
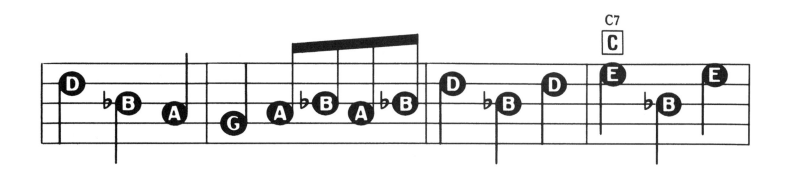

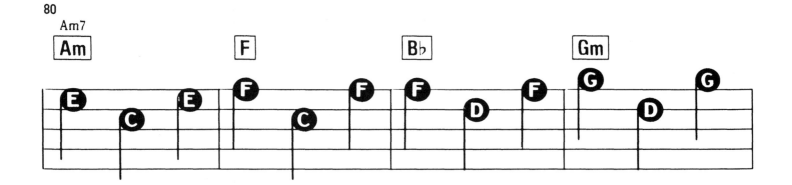

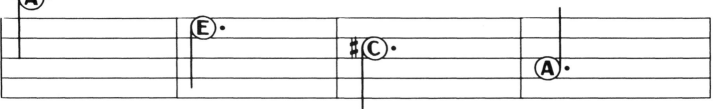

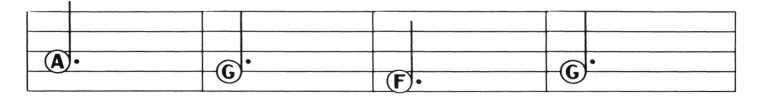

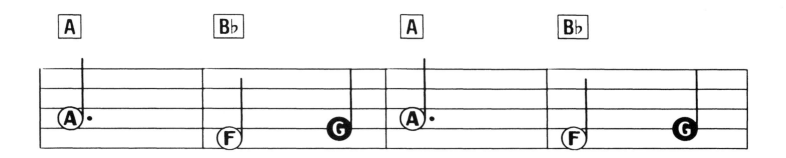

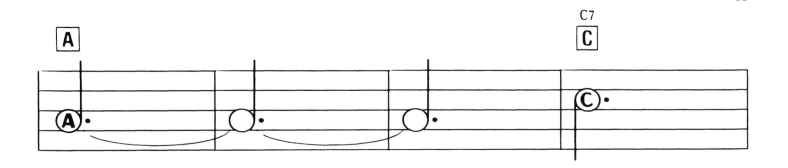

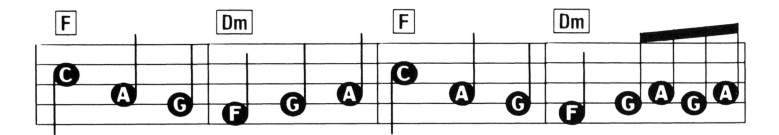

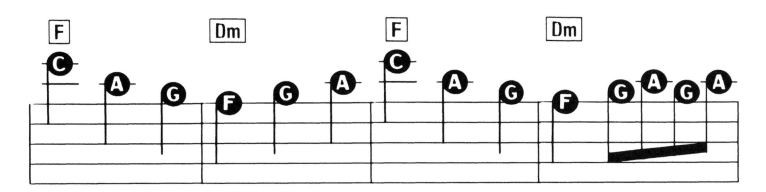

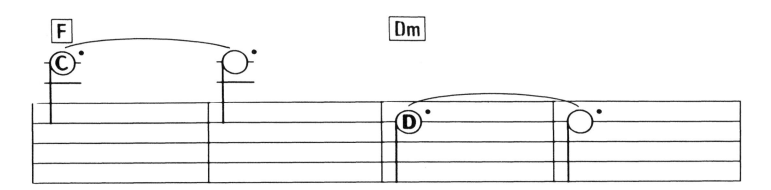

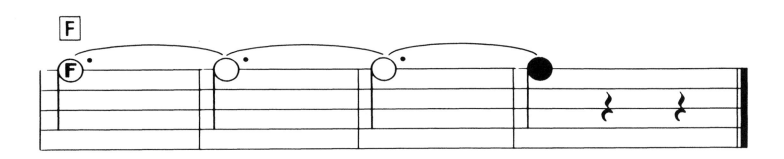

Panis angelicus
(O Lord Most Holy)

Registration 1
Rhythm: None

By César Franck

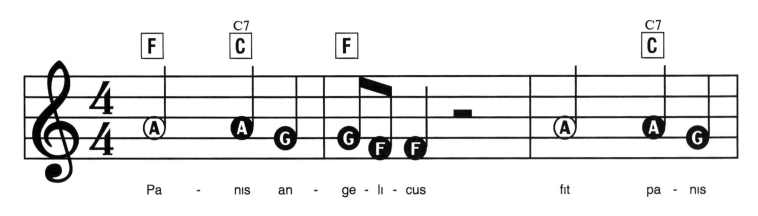

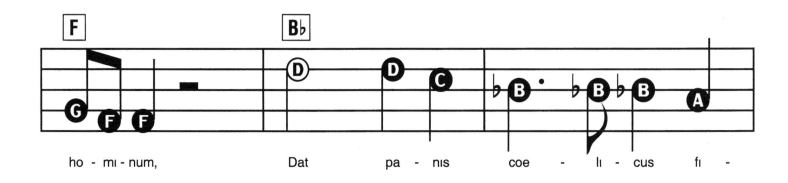

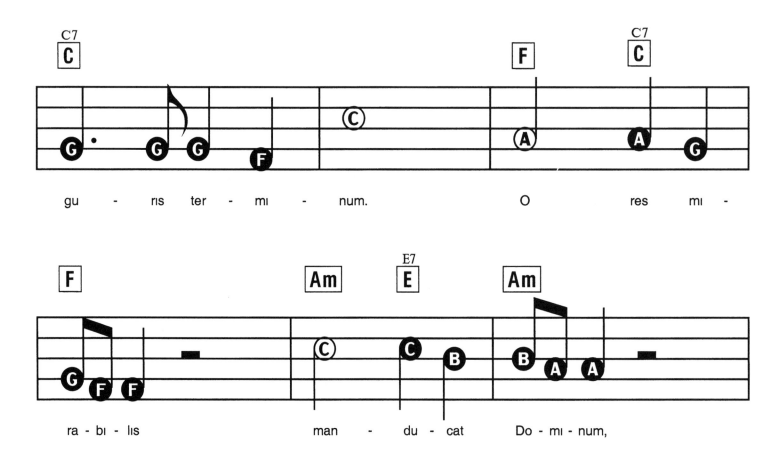

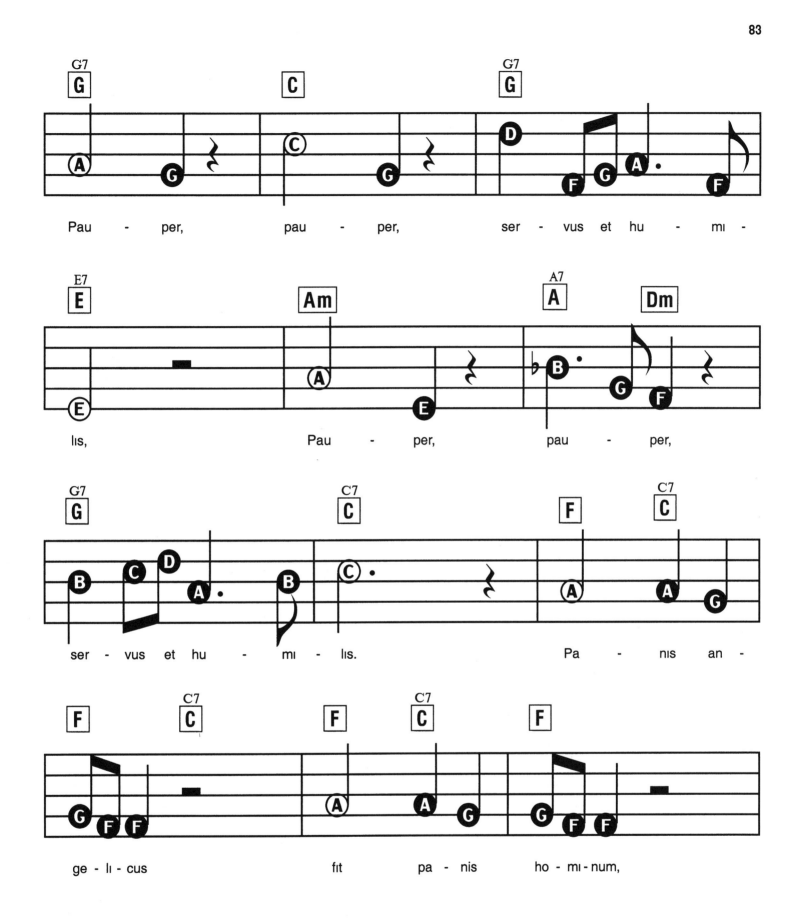

Pau - per, pau - per, ser - vus et hu - mi -

lis, Pau - per, pau - per,

ser - vus et hu - mi - lis. Pa - nis an -

ge - li - cus fit pa - nis ho - mi - num,

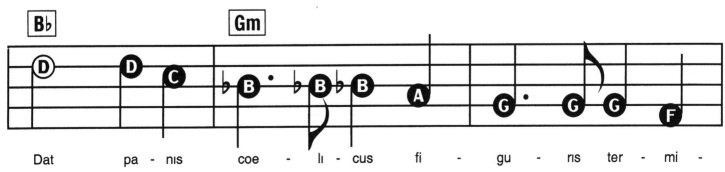

Dat pa - nis coe - li - cus fi - gu - ris ter - mi -

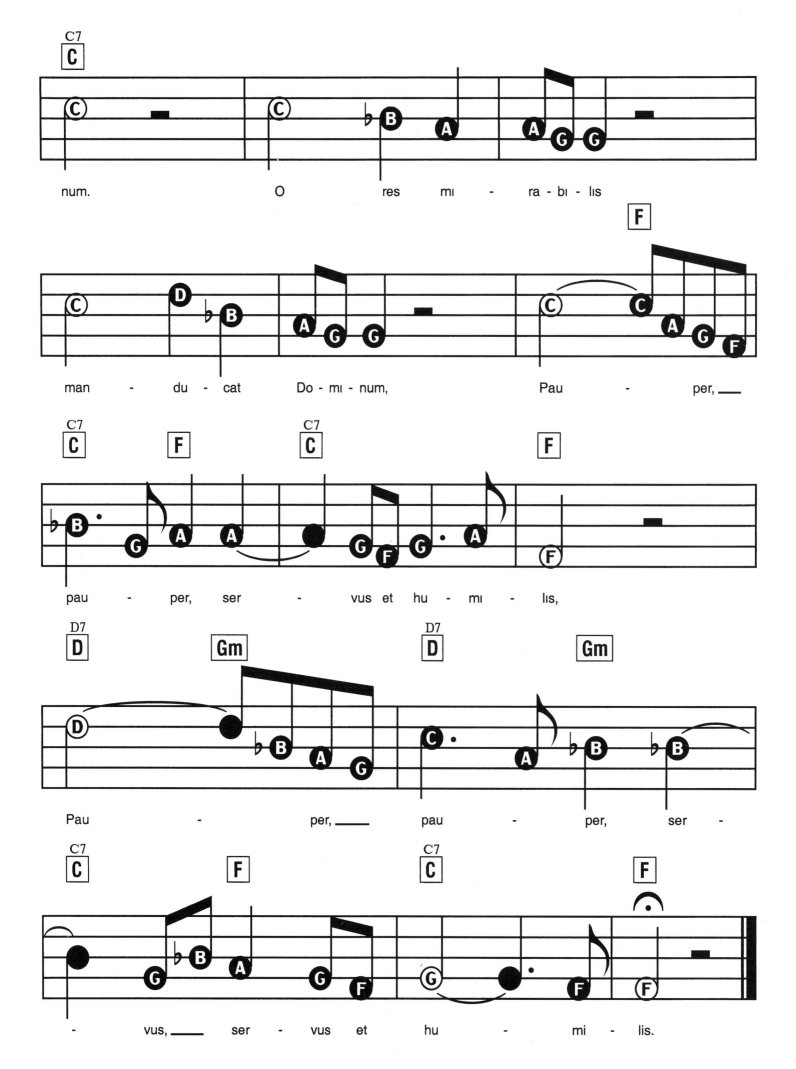

Pizzicato Polka

Registration 10
Rhythm: Polka or March

By Léo Delibes

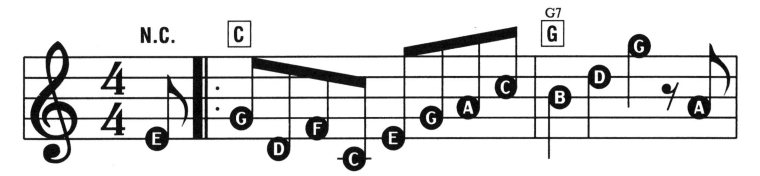

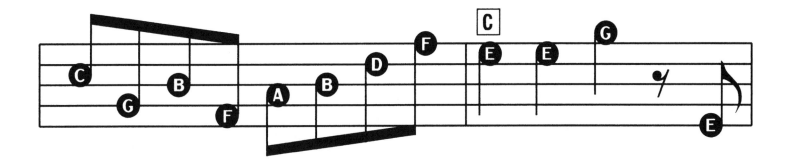

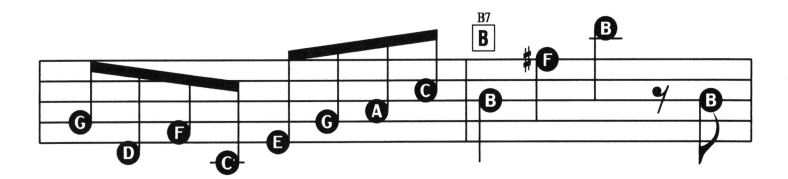

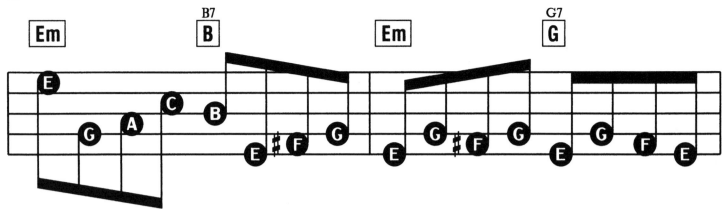

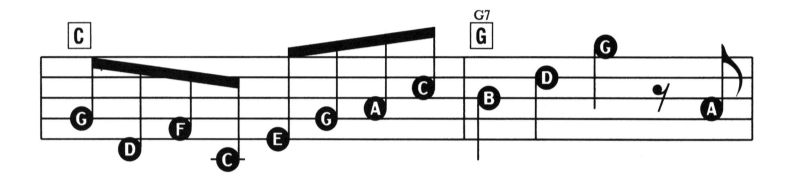

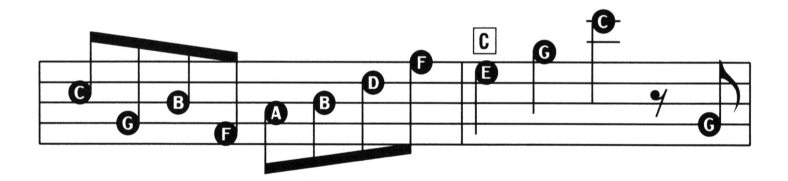

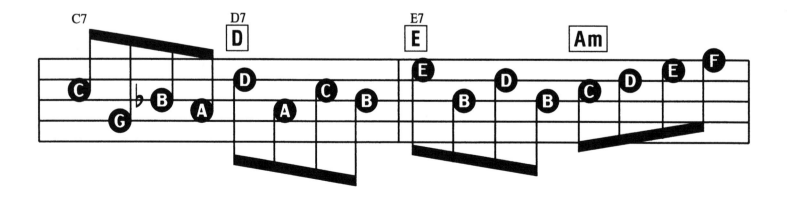

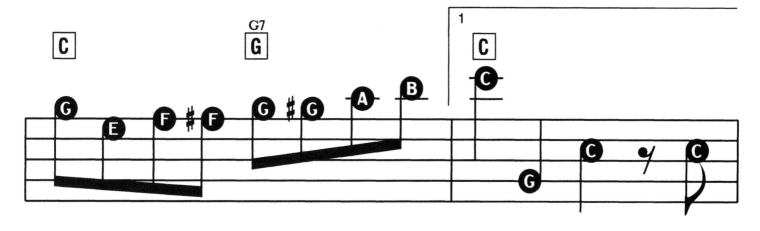

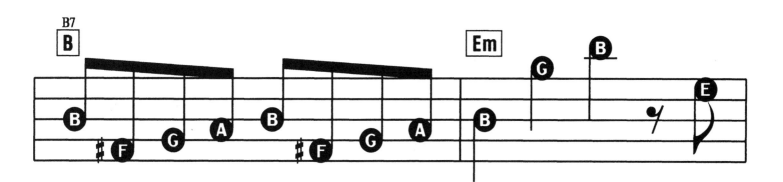

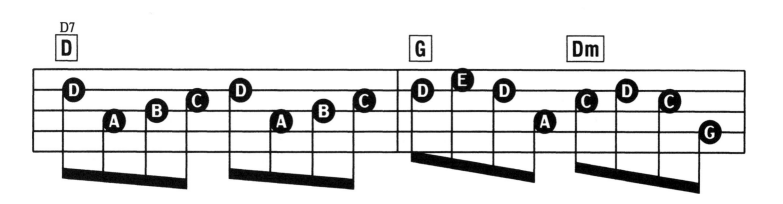

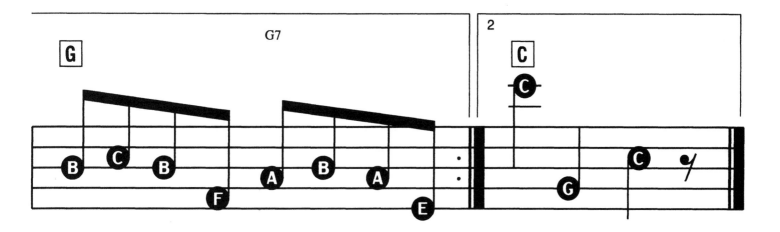

Pilgrims' Chorus
from TANNHÄUSER

Registration 5
Rhythm: Waltz or None

By Richard Wagner

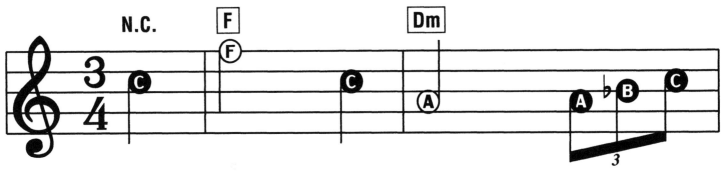

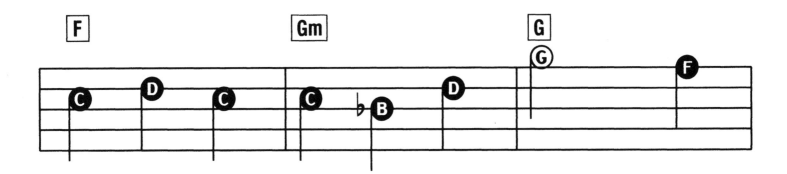

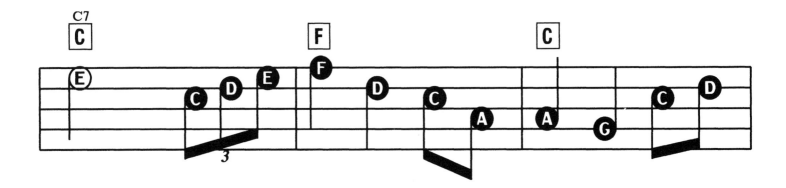

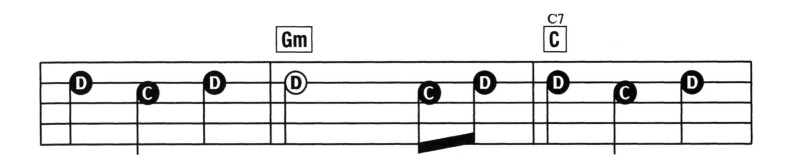

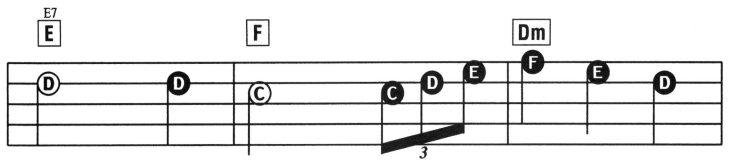

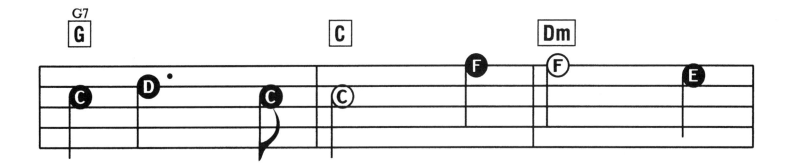

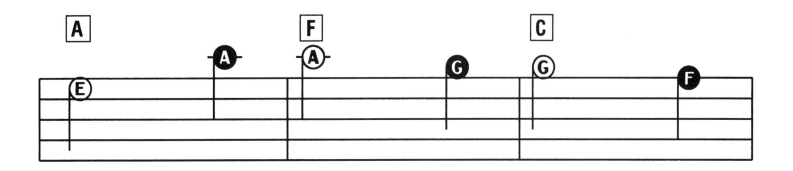

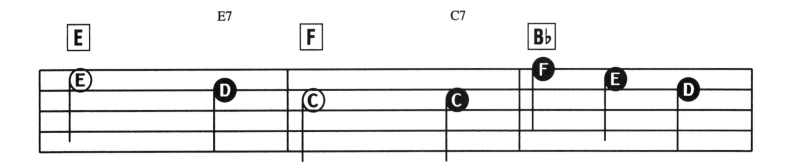

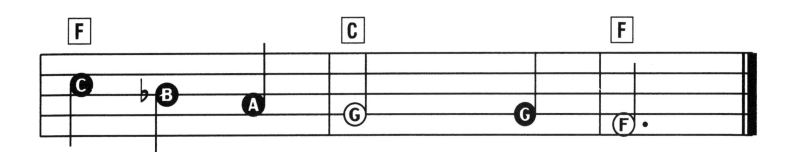

Poet and Peasant Overture

Registration 9
Rhythm: Waltz

By Franz von Suppe

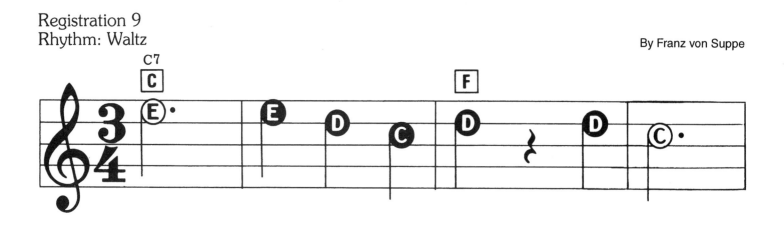

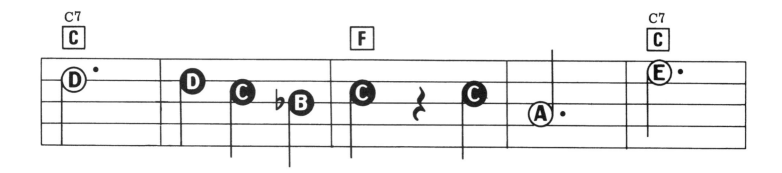

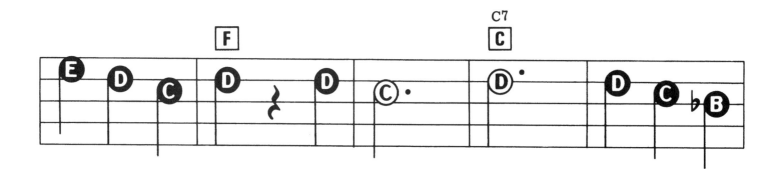

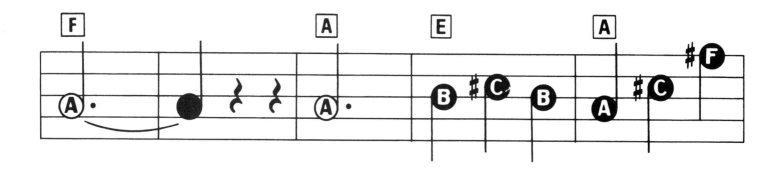

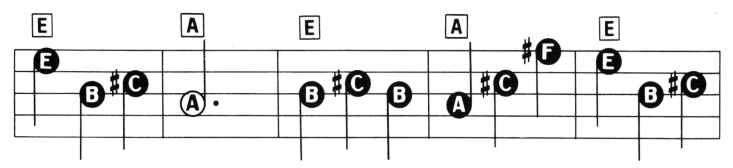

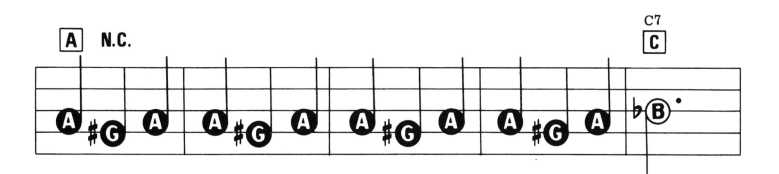

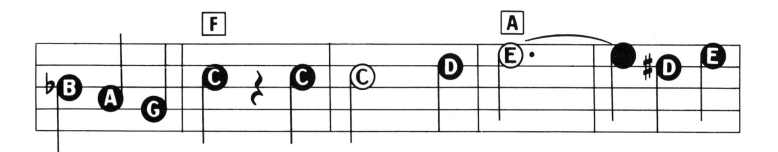

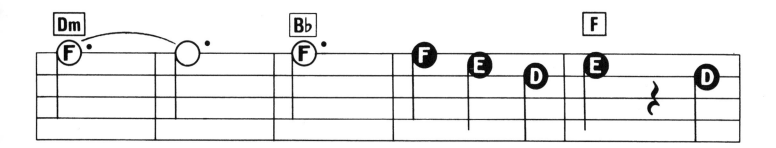

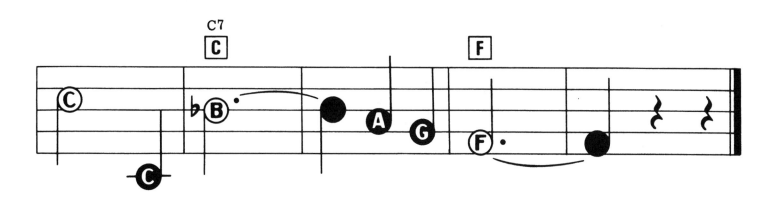

Polovetzian Dance
from PRINCE IGOR

Registration 9
Rhythm: Fox Trot

By Alexander Borodin

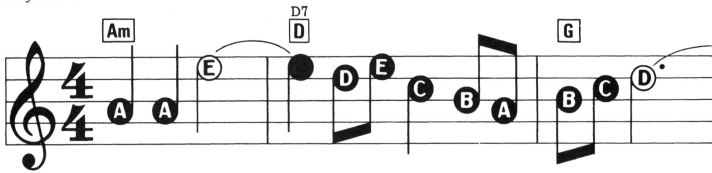

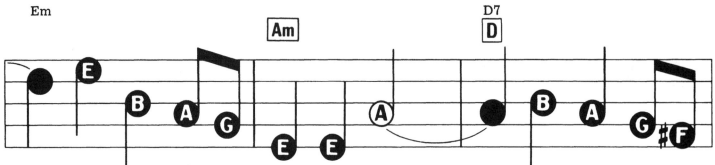

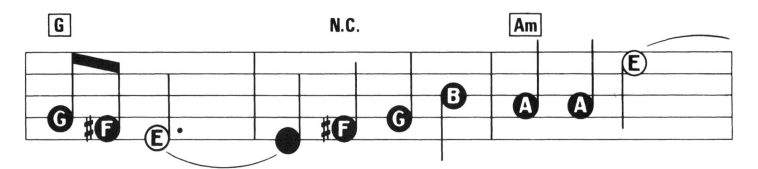

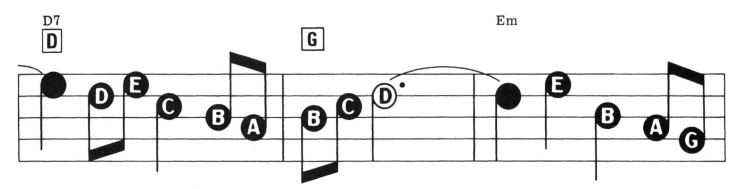

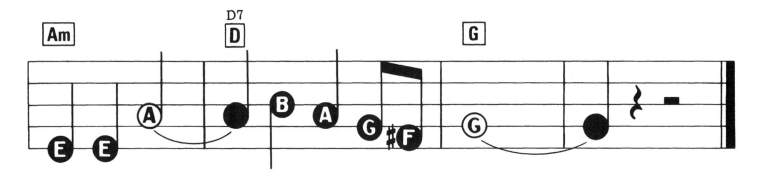

Prelude, Op. 28, No. 7

Registration 10
Rhythm: Waltz

By Fryderyk Chopin

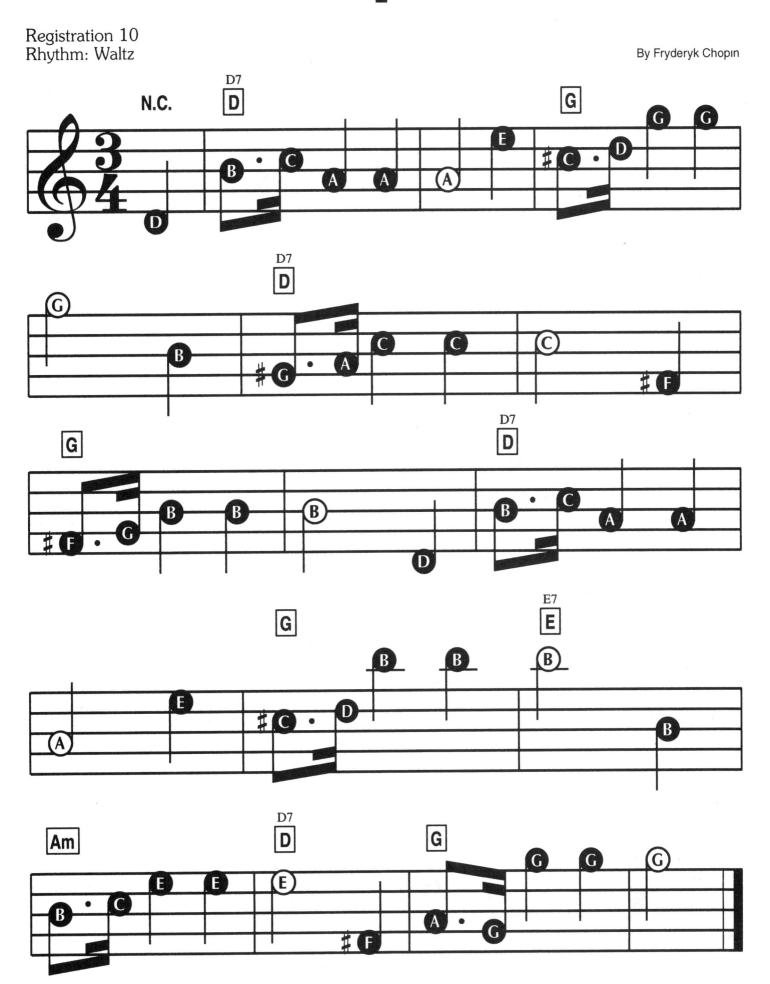

Quando men vo
(Musetta's Waltz)
from LA BOHÈME

Registration 3
Rhythm: Waltz

By Giacomo Puccini

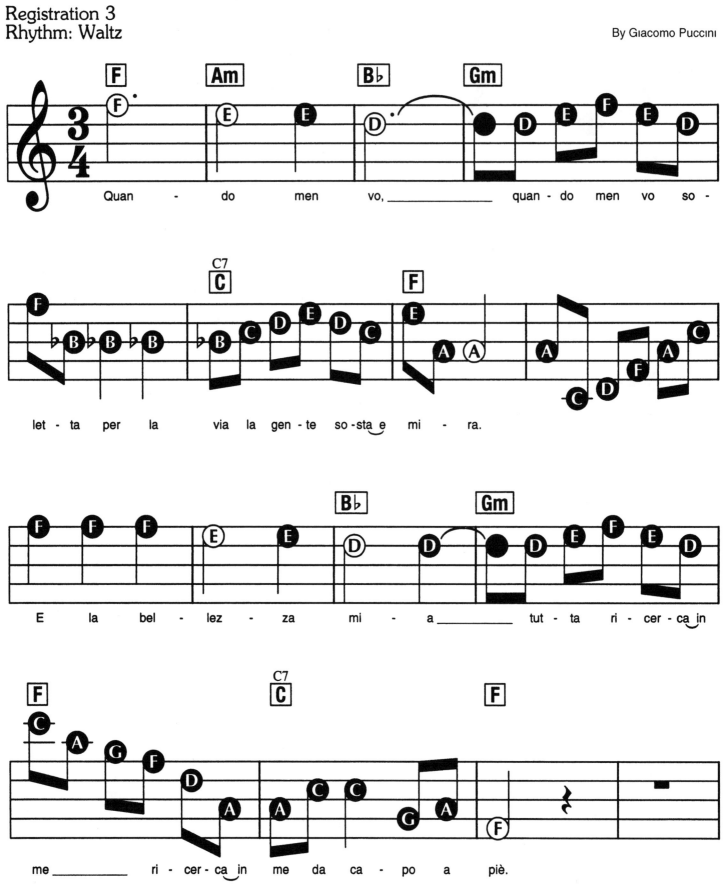

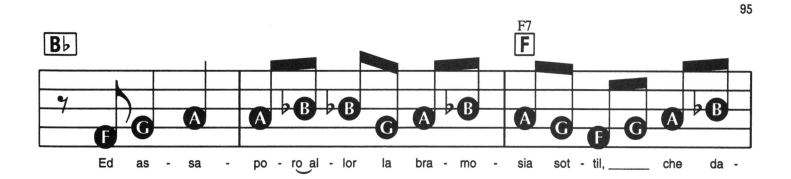

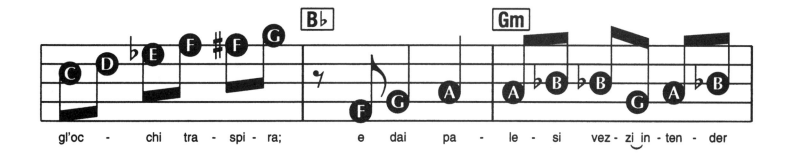

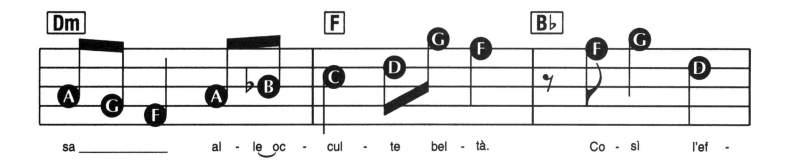

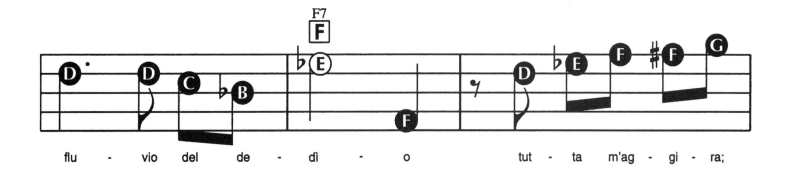

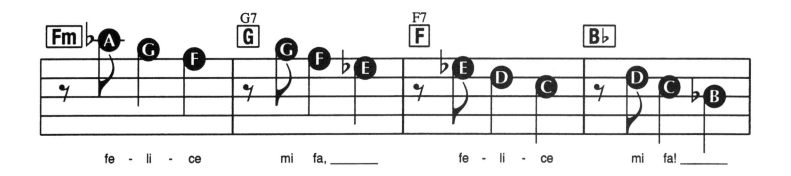

96

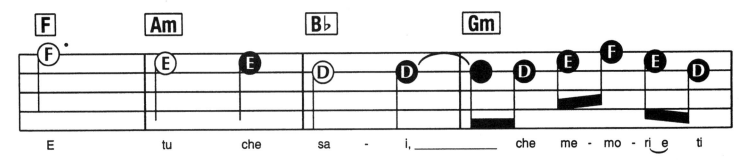

E tu che sa - i, ___ che me - mo - ri e ti

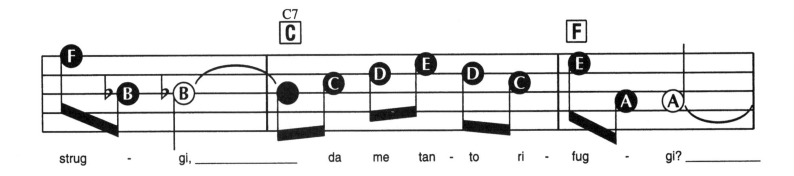

strug - gi, ___ da me tan - to ri - fug - gi? ___

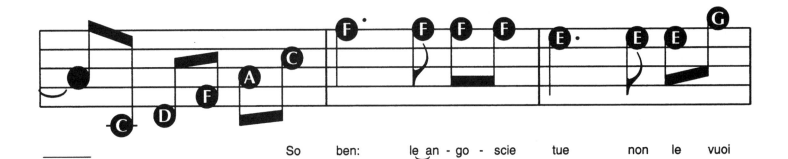

So ben: le an - go - scie tue non le vuoi

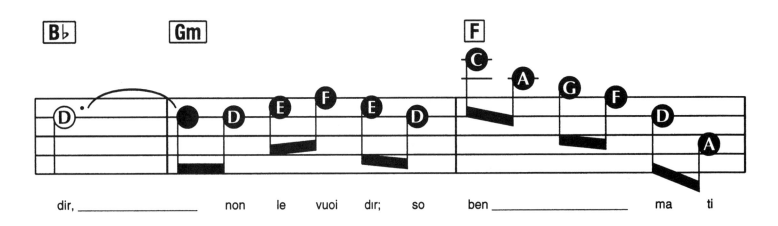

dir, ___ non le vuoi dir; so ben ___ ma ti

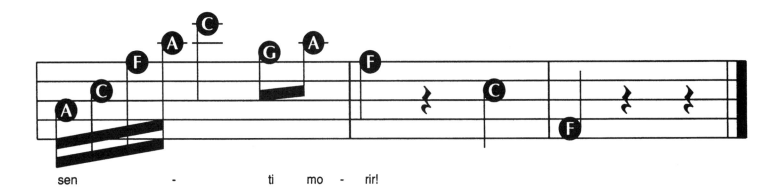

sen - ti mo - rir!

Sheep May Safely Graze

from CANTATA NO. 208

Registration 1
Rhythm: None

By Johann Sebastian Bach

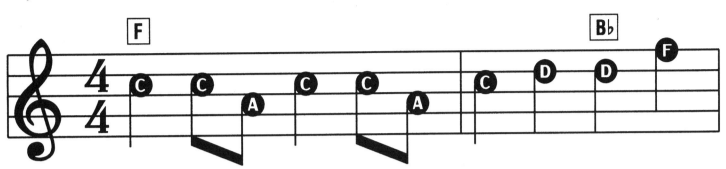

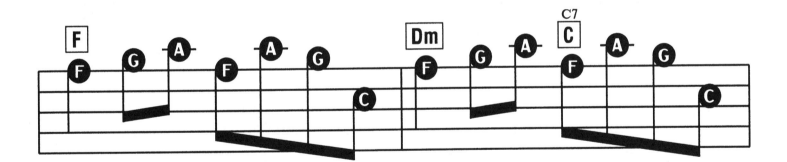

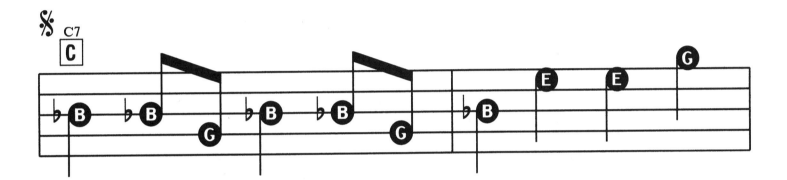

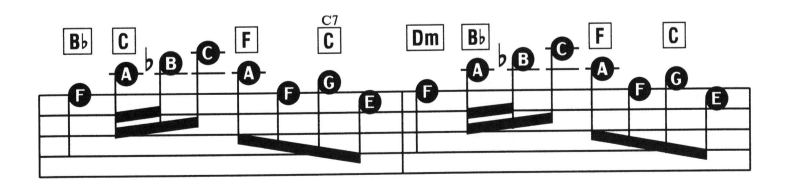

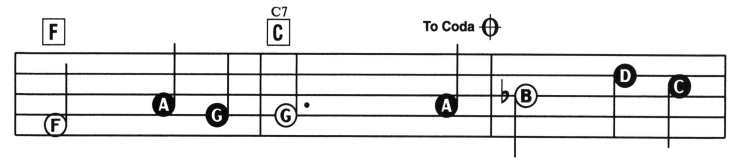

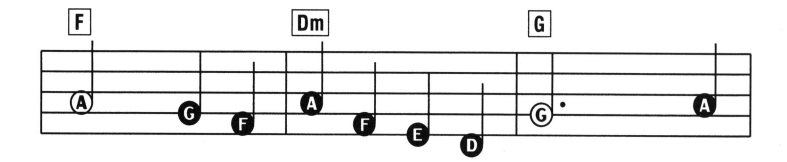

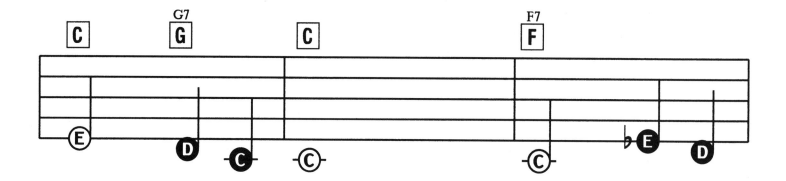

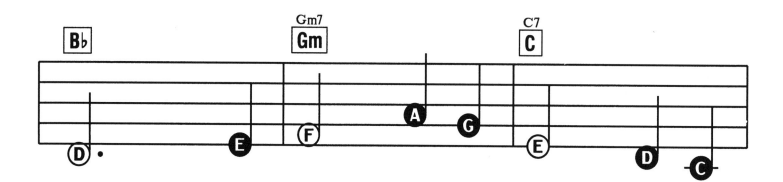

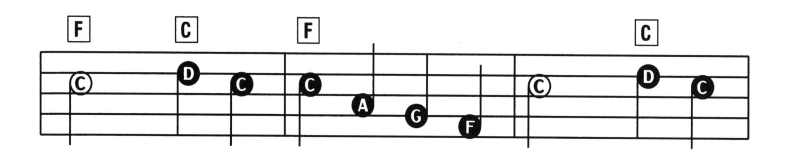

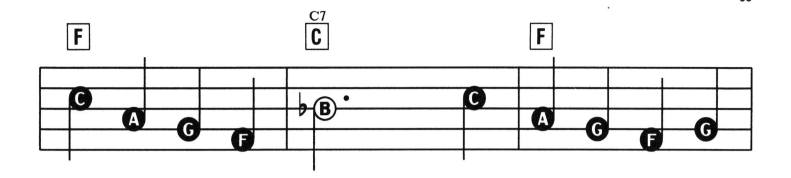

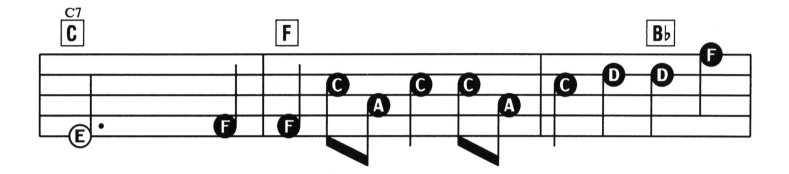

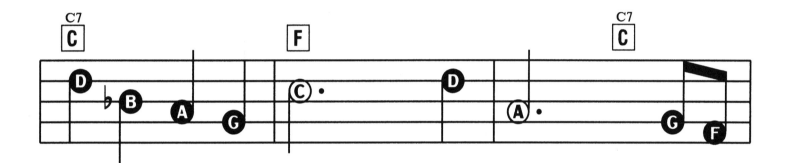

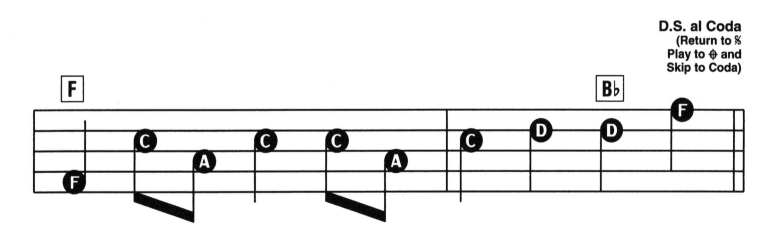

D.S. al Coda
(Return to %
Play to ⊕ and
Skip to Coda)

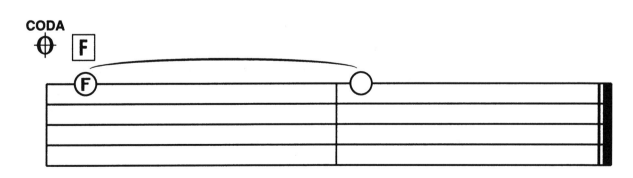

Rêverie

Registration 8
Rhythm: 8 Beat or None

By Claude Debussy

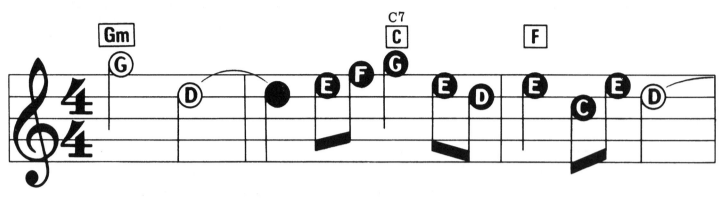

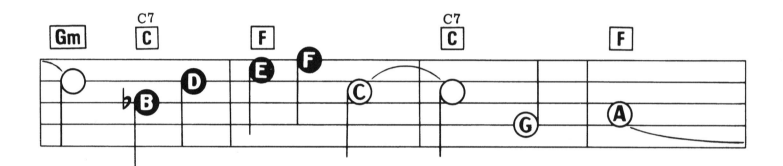

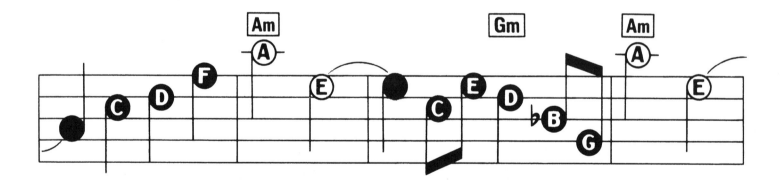

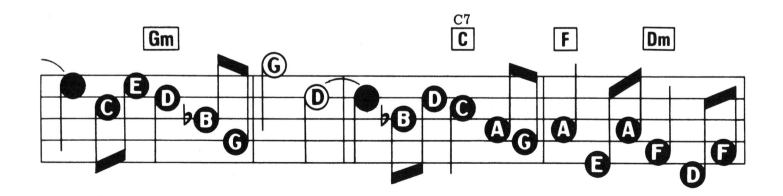

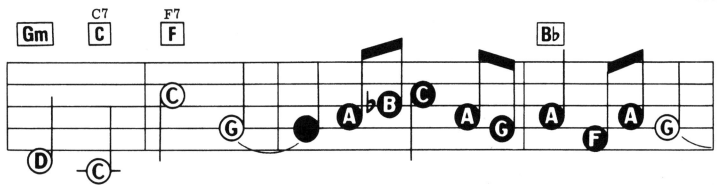

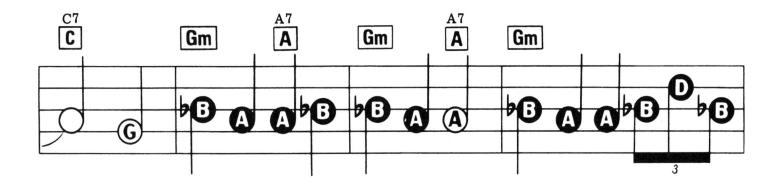

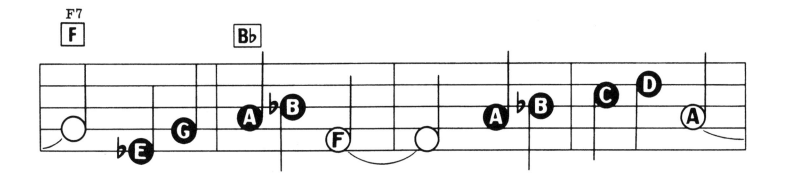

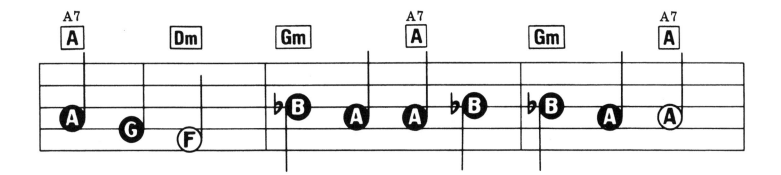

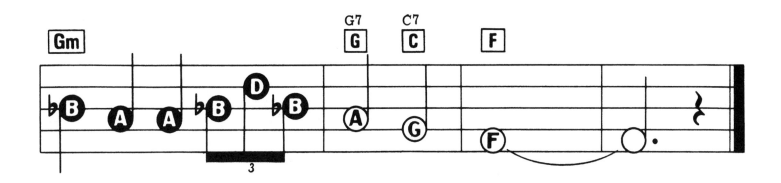

Ride of the Valkyries
from DIE WALKÜRE

Registration 5
Rhythm: Waltz

By Richard Wagner

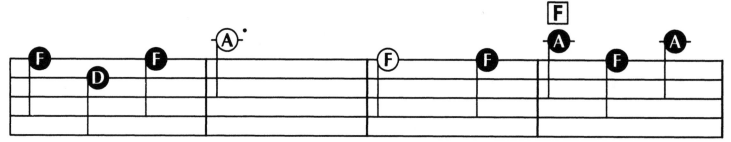

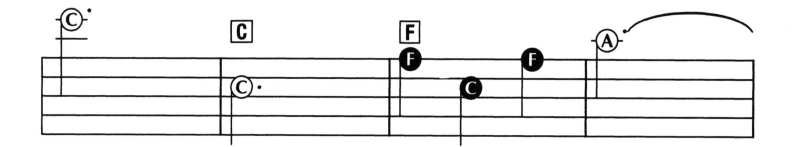

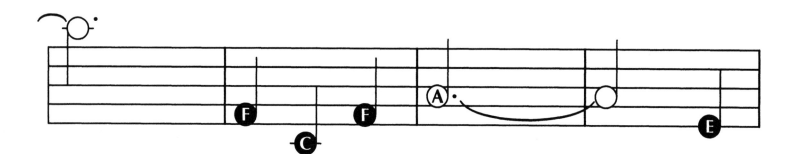

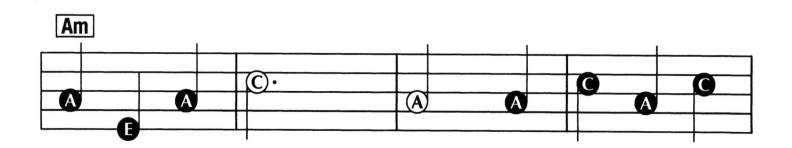

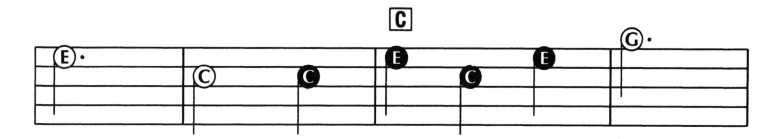

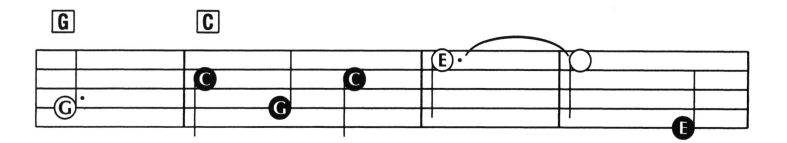

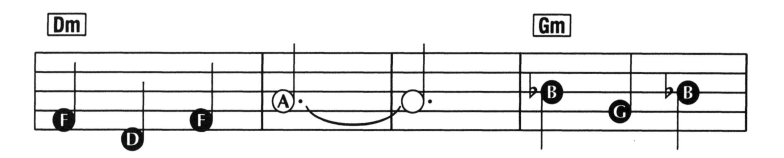

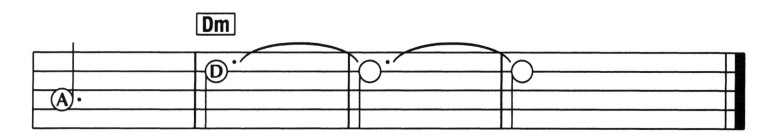

Romeo and Juliet
(Love Theme)

Registration 3
Rhythm: None

By Pyotr Il'yich Tchaikovsky

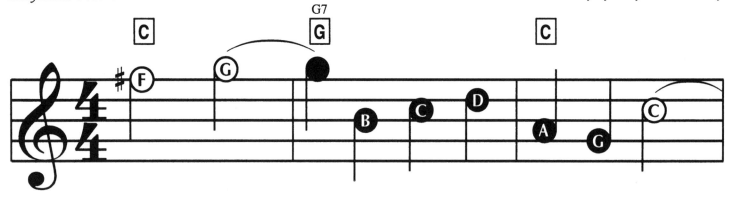

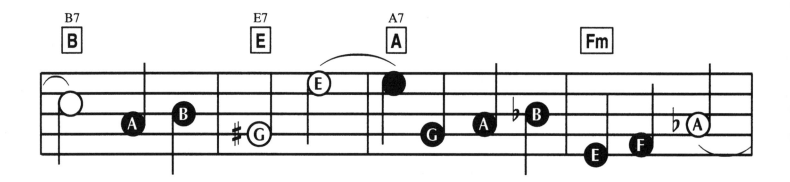

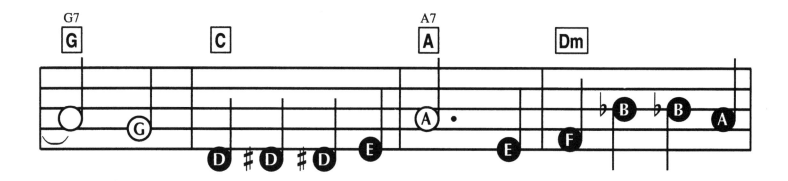

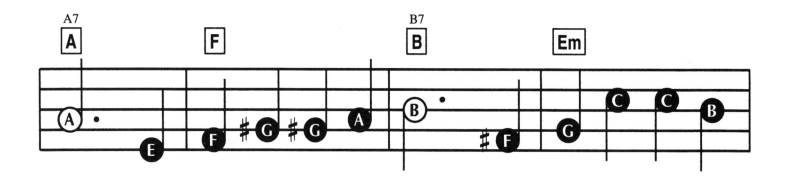

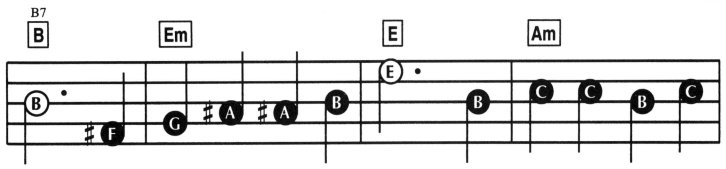

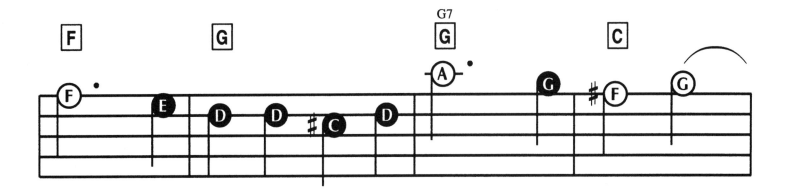

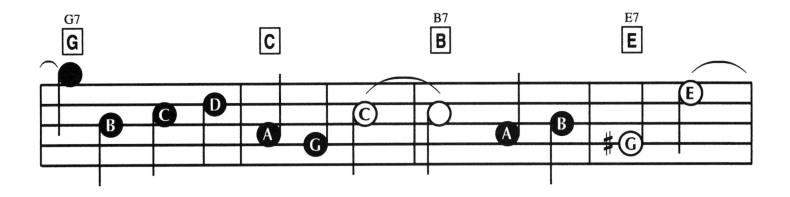

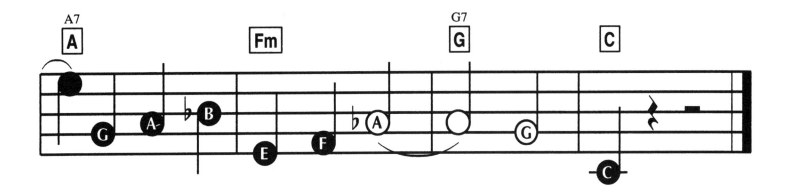

Roses from the South

Registration 3
Rhythm: Waltz

By Johann Strauss

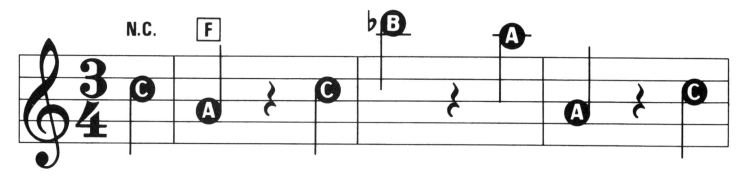

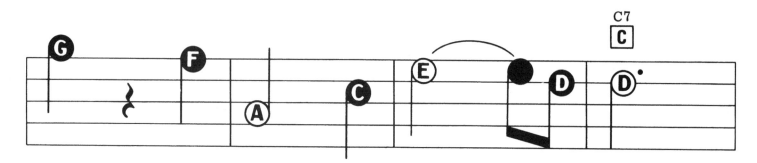

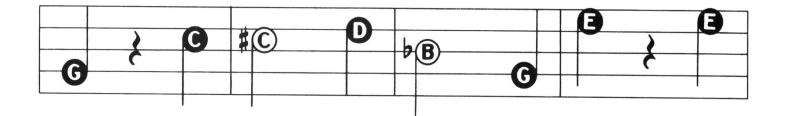

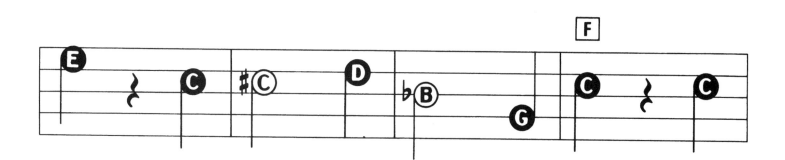

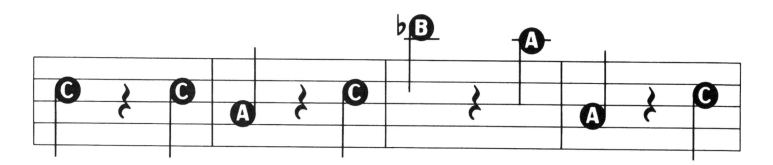

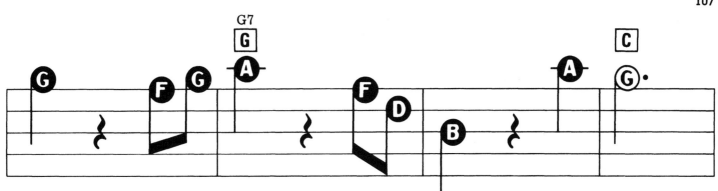

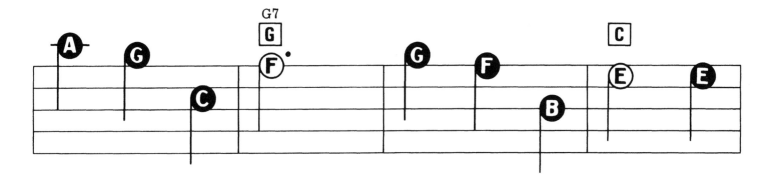

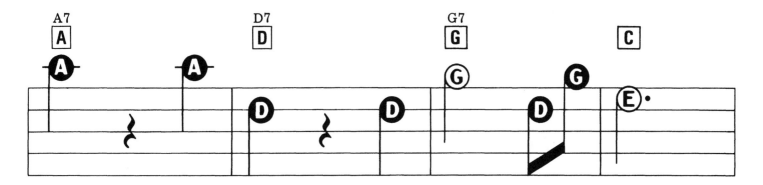

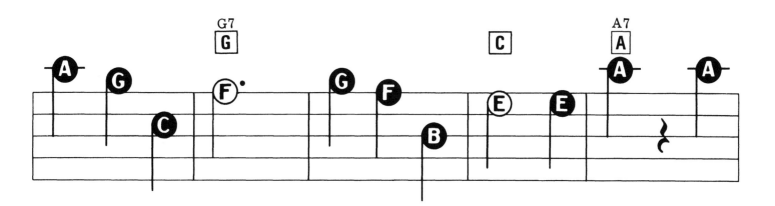

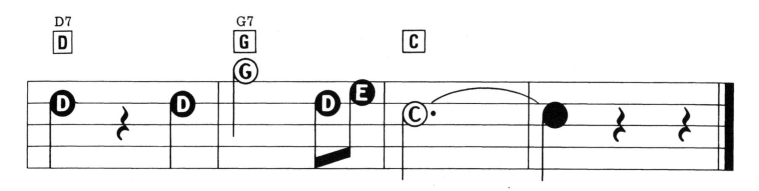

Sheherazade
Theme from Part Three

Registration 10
Rhythm: Waltz

By Nikolay Rimsky-Korsakov

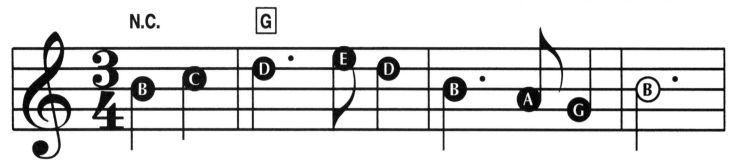

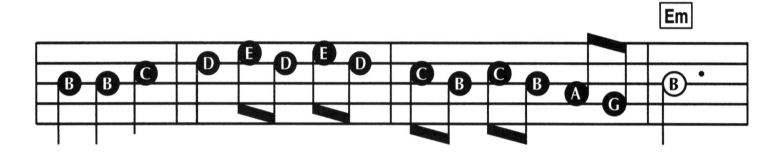

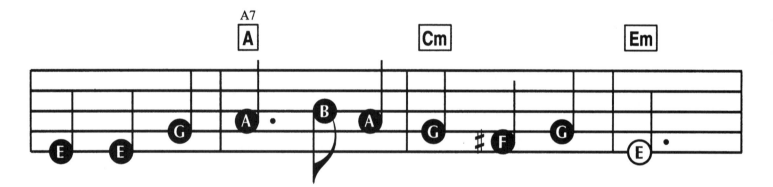

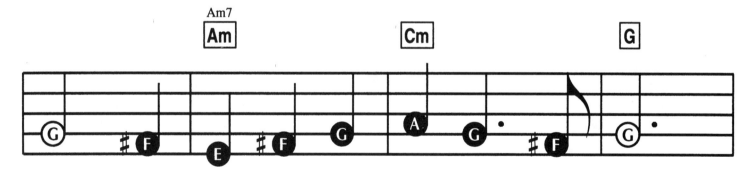

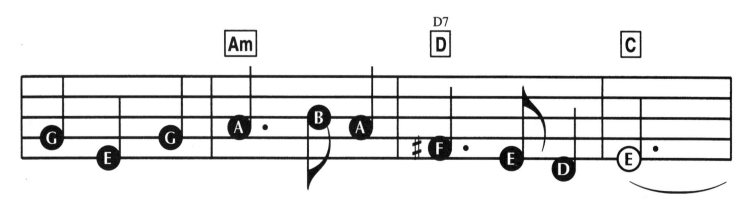

109

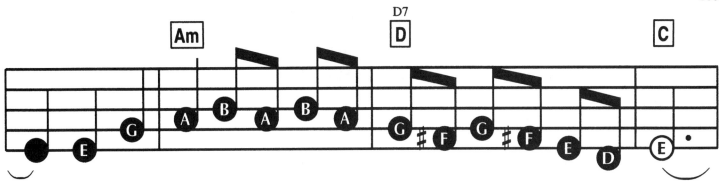

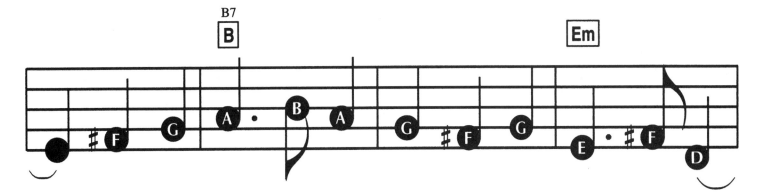

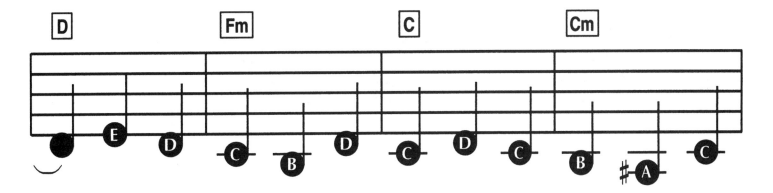

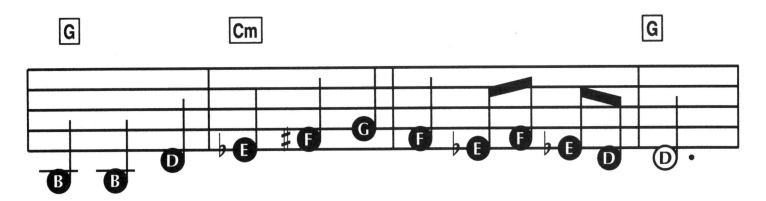

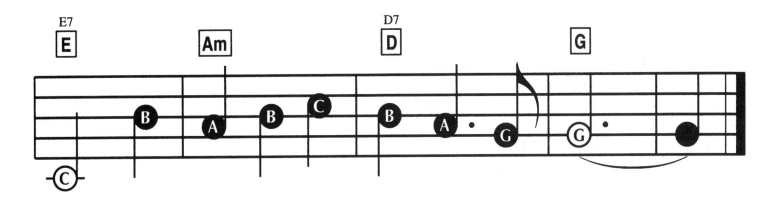

Symphony No. 8
"Unfinished"
First Movement Theme

Registration 3
Rhythm: Waltz

By Franz Schubert

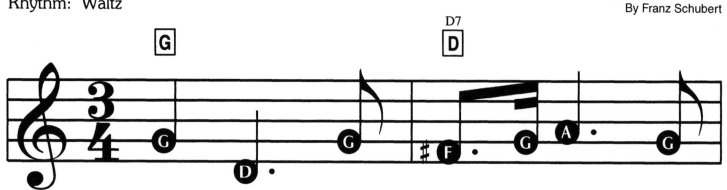

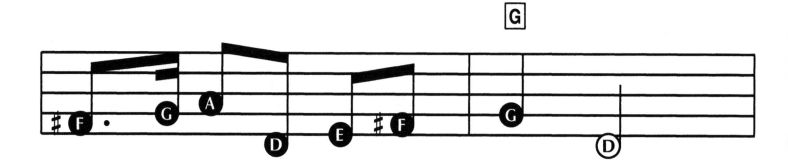

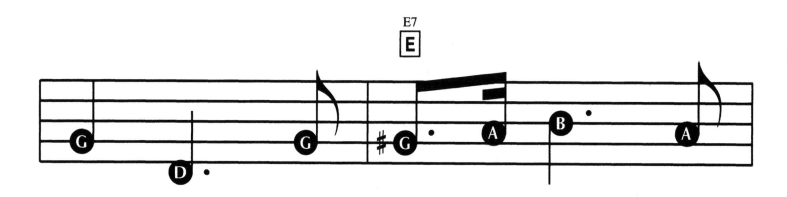

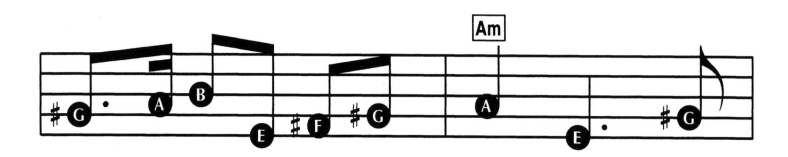

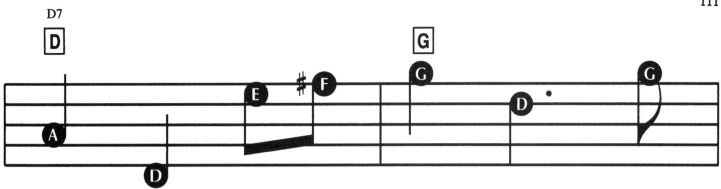

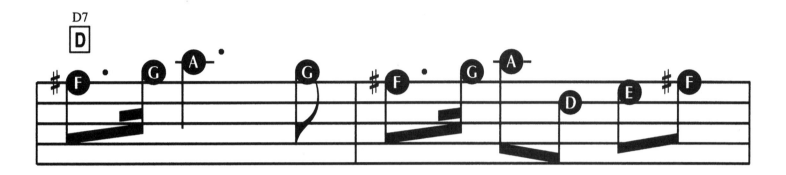

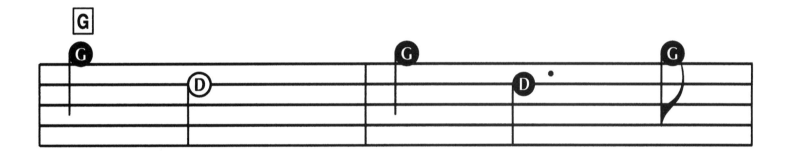

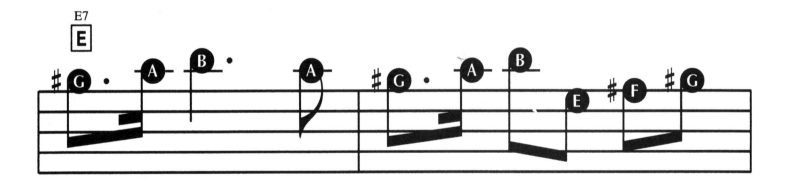

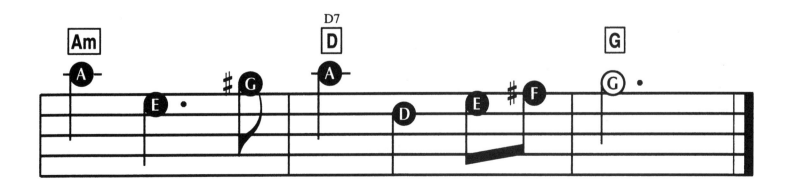

Symphony No. 9 in E Minor
"From the New World"
Second Movement Excerpt

Registration 7
Rhythm: None

By Antonín Dvořák

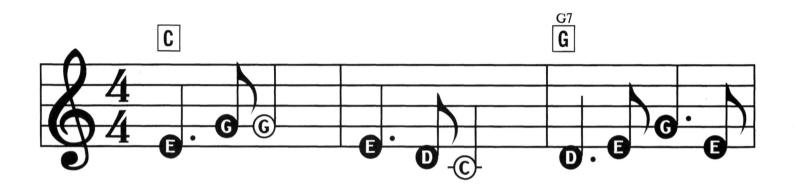

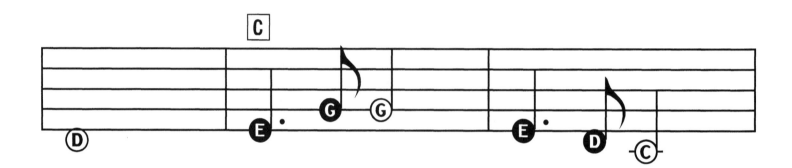

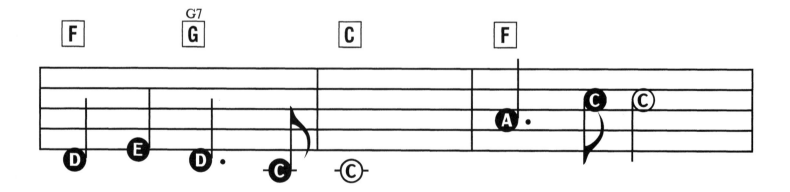

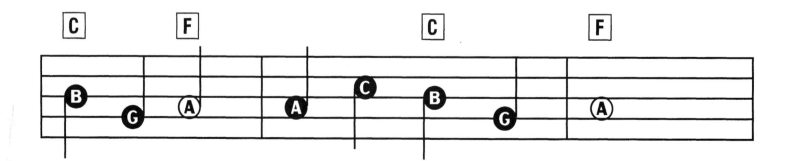

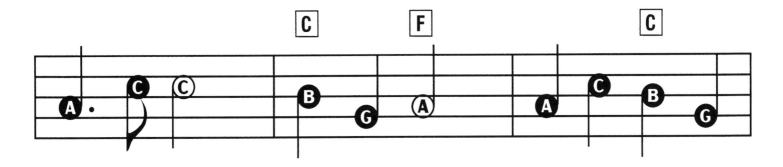

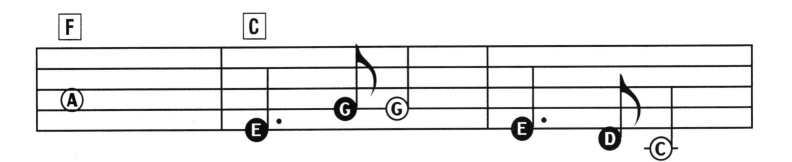

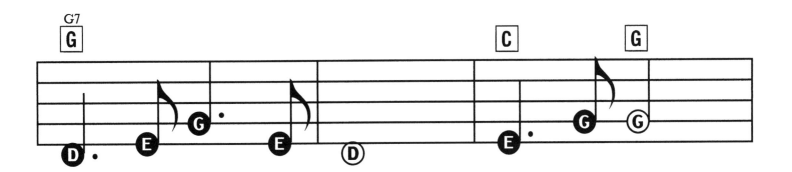

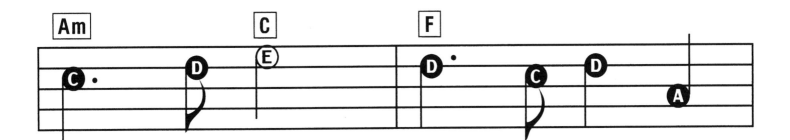

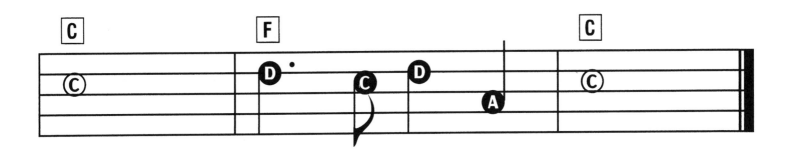

Surprise Symphony
Second Movement Theme

Registration 5
Rhythm: None

By Franz Joseph Haydn

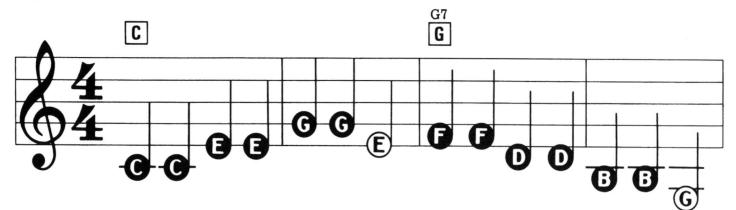

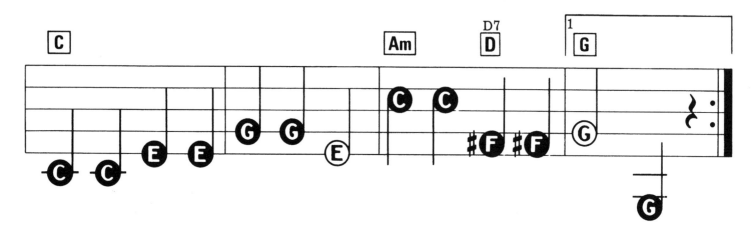

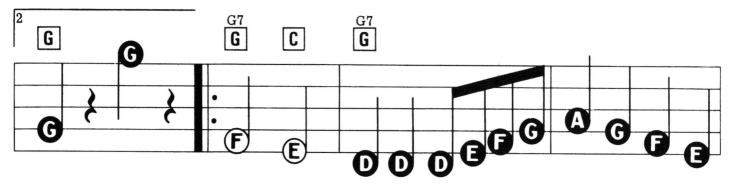

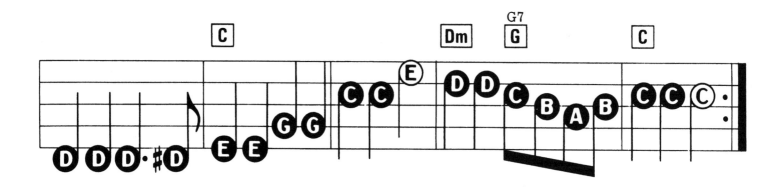

Una furtiva lagrima

from L'ELISIR D'AMORE (THE ELIXIR OF LOVE)

Registration 1
Rhythm: Waltz or None

By Gaetano Donizetti

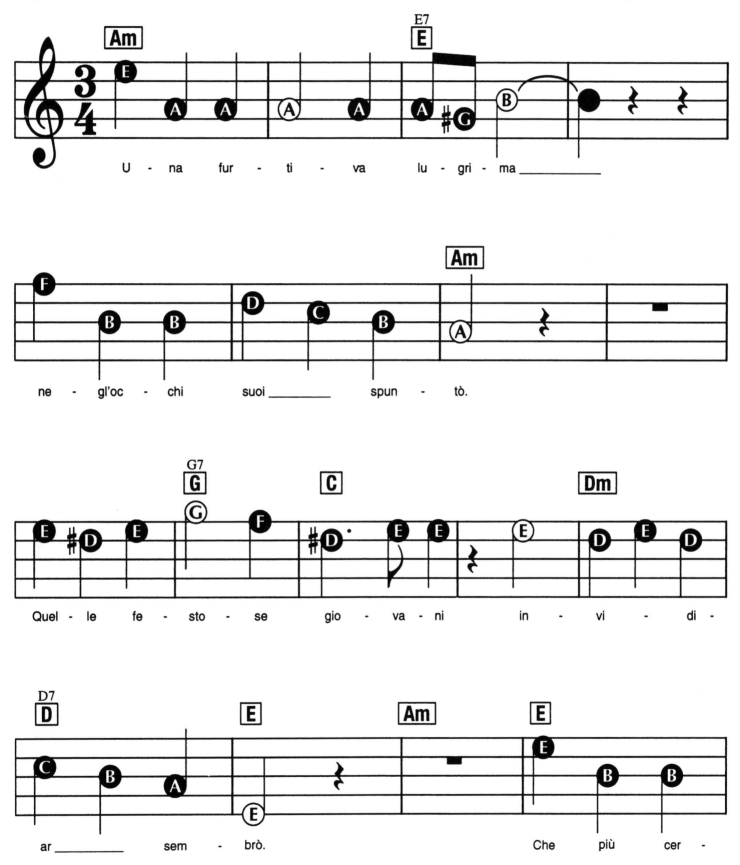

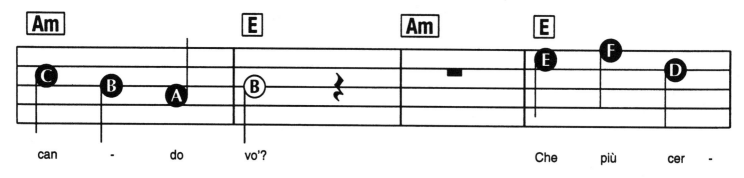

can - do vo'? Che più cer -

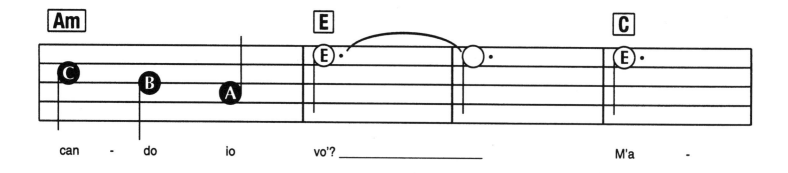

can - do io vo'? _____ M'a -

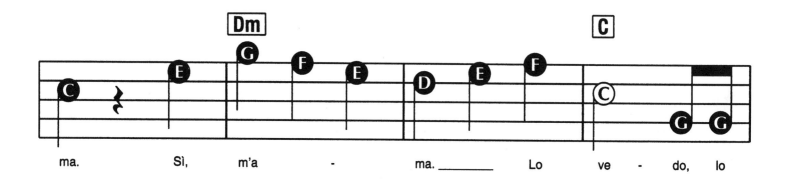

ma. Sì, m'a - ma. _____ Lo ve - do, lo

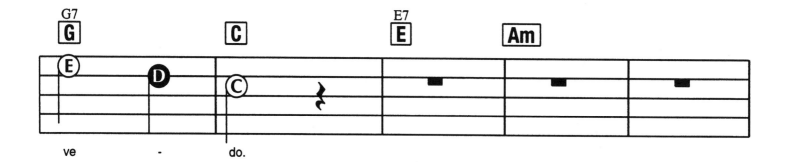

ve - do.

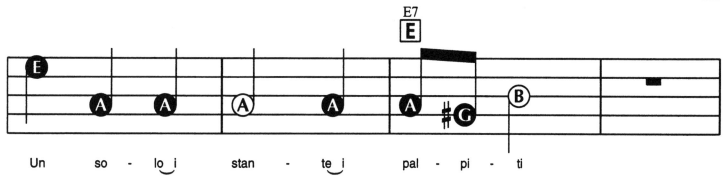

Un so - lo i stan - te i pal - pi - ti

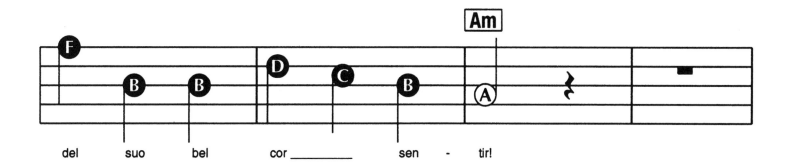

del suo bel cor _____ sen - tir!

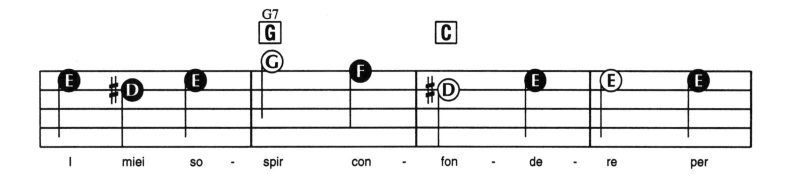

I miei so - spir con - fon - de - re per

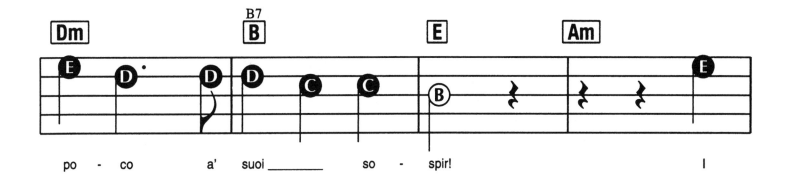

po - co a' suoi _____ so - spir!   I

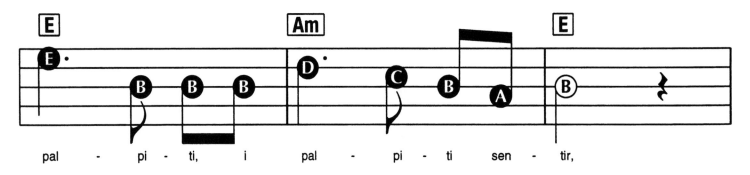

pal - pi - ti, i pal - pi - ti sen - tir,

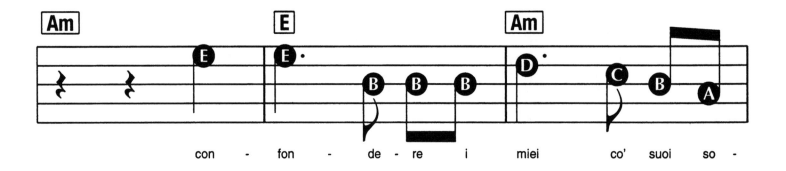

con - fon - de - re i miei co' suoi so -

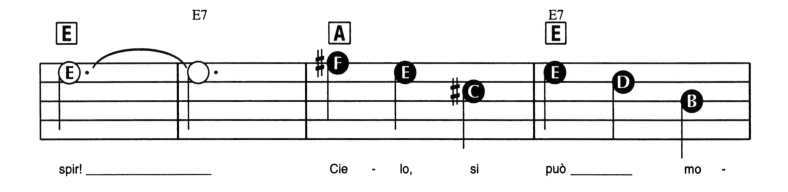

spir! _____ Cie - lo, si può _____ mo -

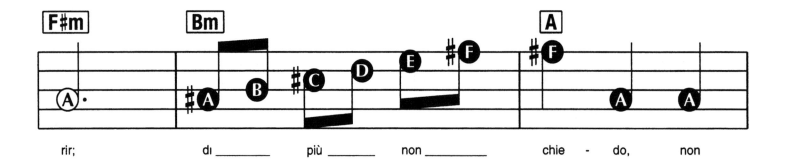

rir; di _____ più _____ non _____ chie - do, non

119

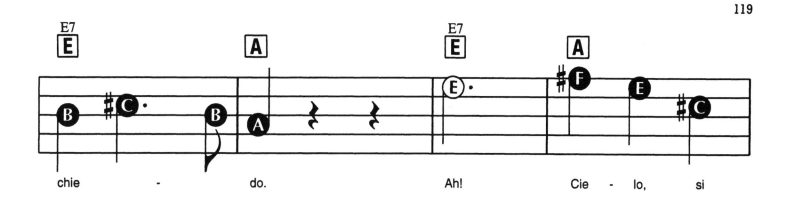

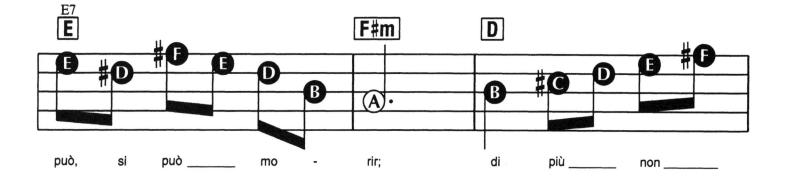

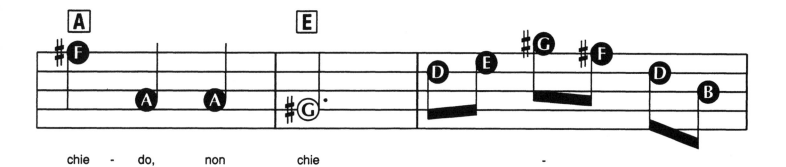

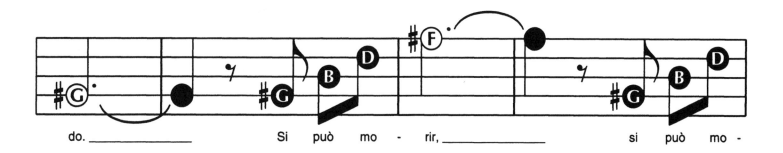

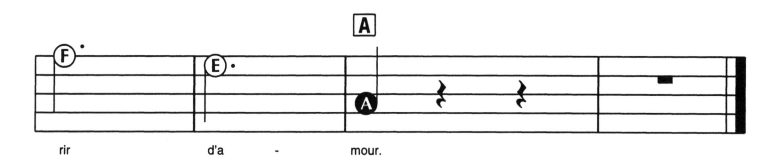

Tales from the Vienna Woods

Registration 4
Rhythm: Waltz

By Johann Strauss, Jr

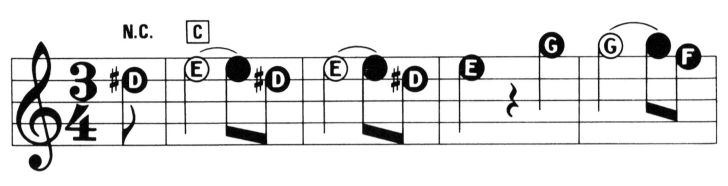

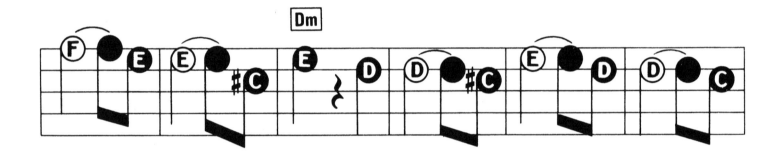

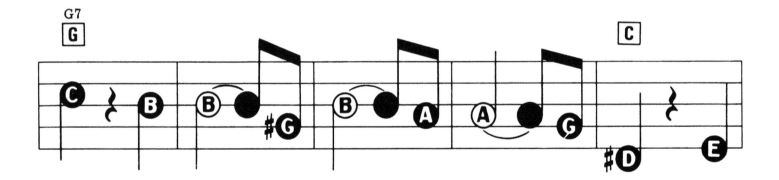

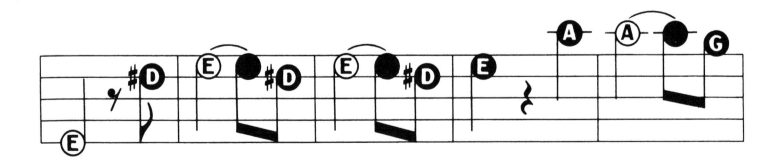

121

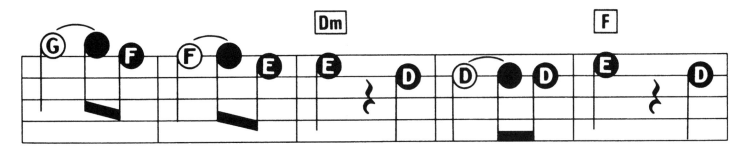
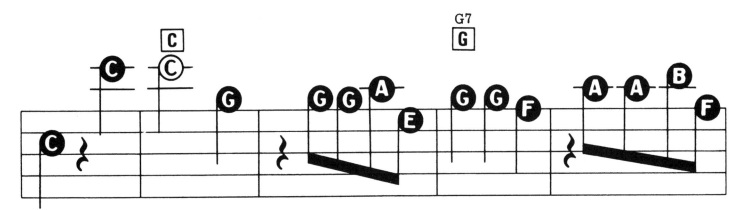
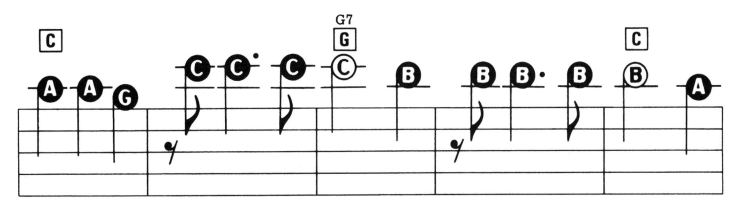
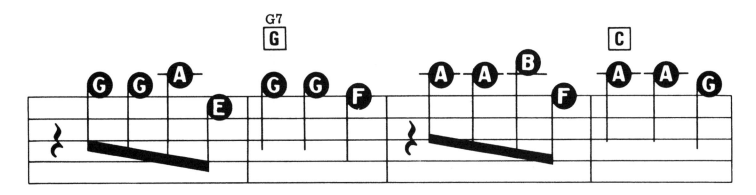
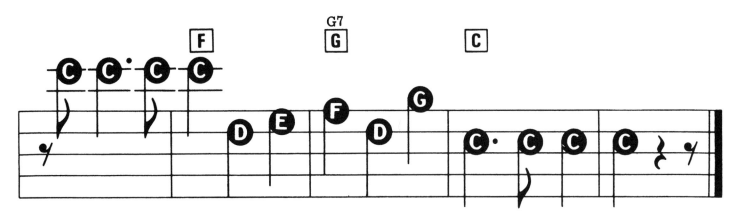

Toccata & Fugue in D Minor

Registration 6
Rhythm: None

By Johann Sebastian Bach

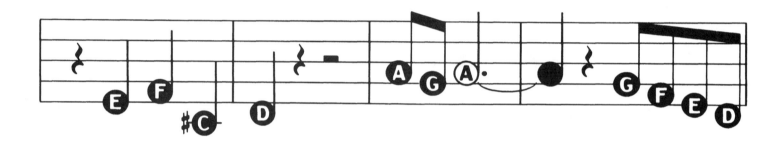

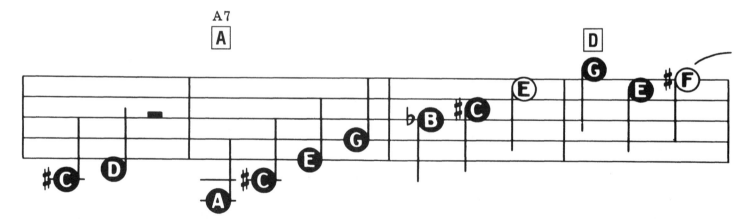

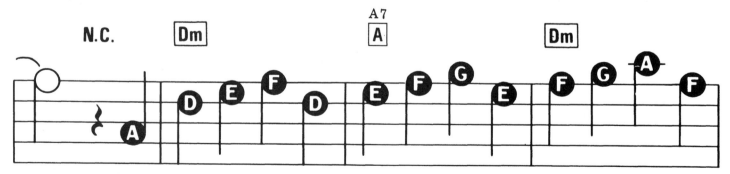

123

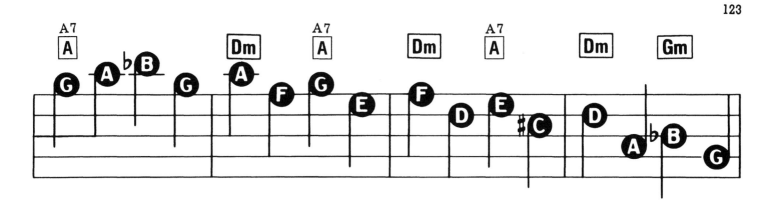

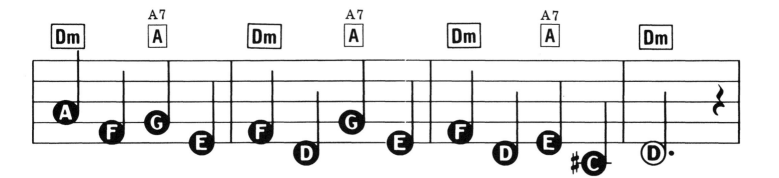

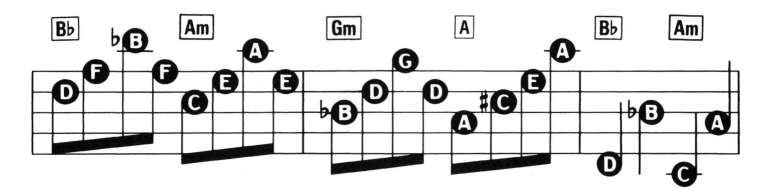

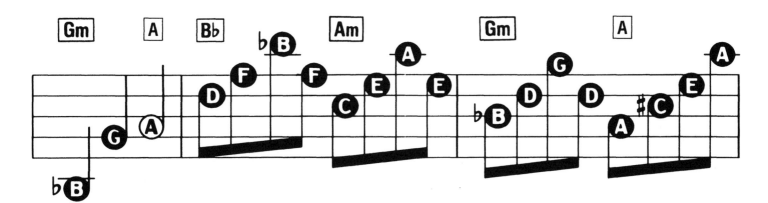

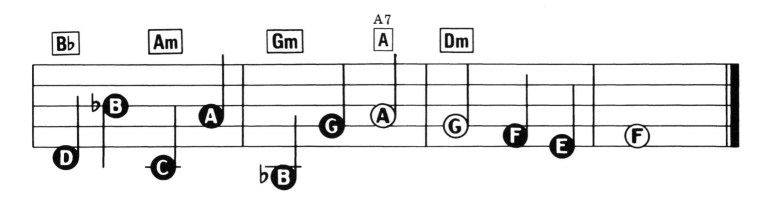

Toreador Song
from CARMEN

Registration 1
Rhythm: March (Optional)

By Georges Bizet

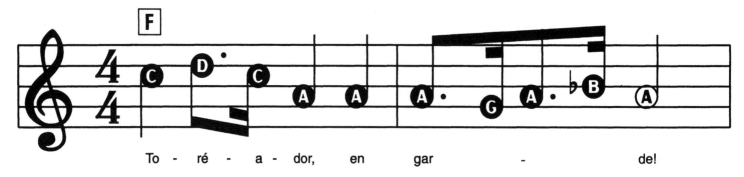

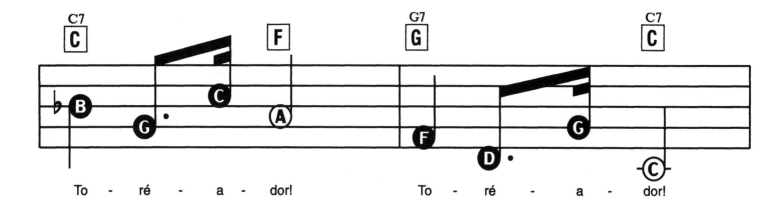

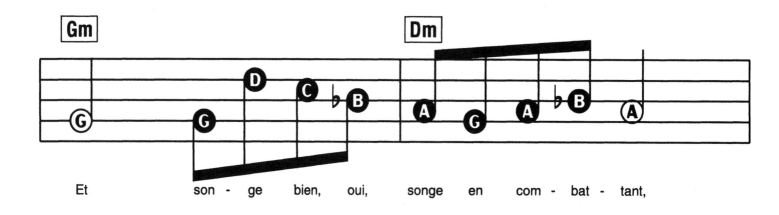

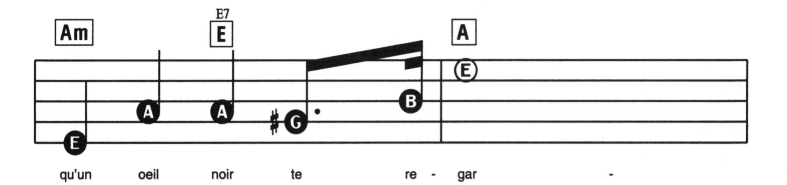

qu'un   oeil   noir   te   re - gar   -

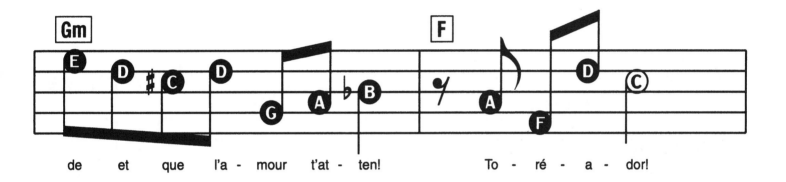

de   et   que   l'a - mour   t'at - ten!   To - ré - a - dor!

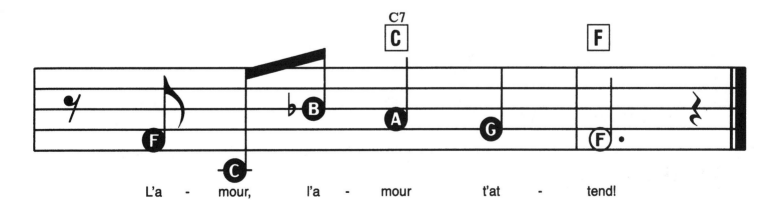

L'a - mour,   l'a - mour   t'at - tend!

Turkish March
from THE RUINS OF ATHENS

Registration 5
Rhythm: March

By Ludwig van Beethoven

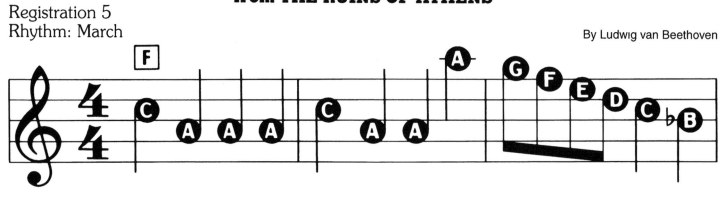

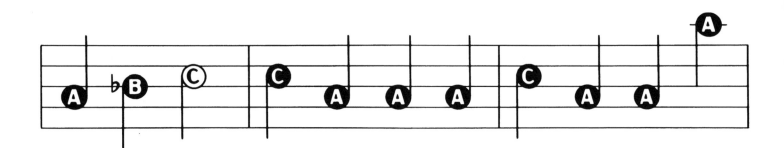

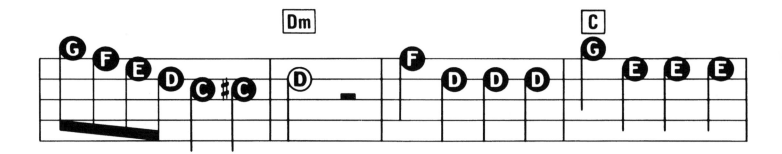

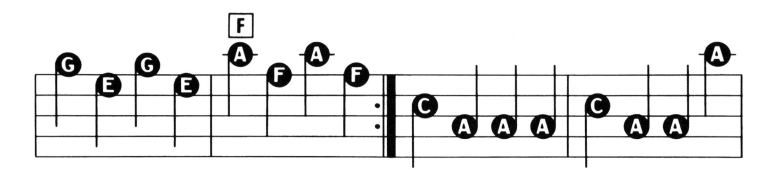

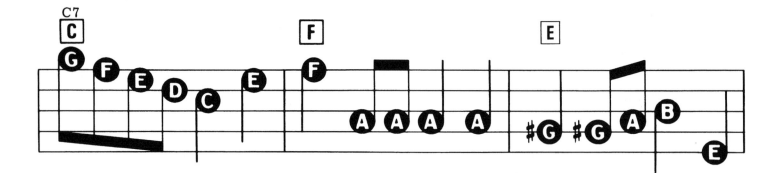

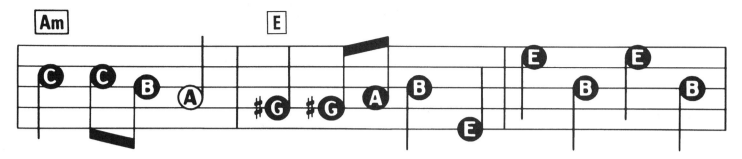

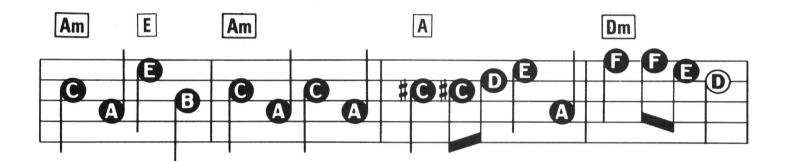

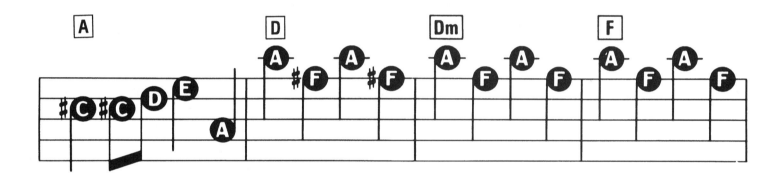

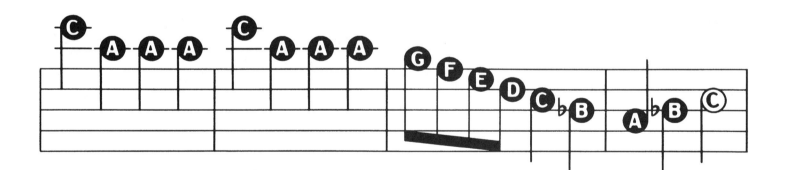

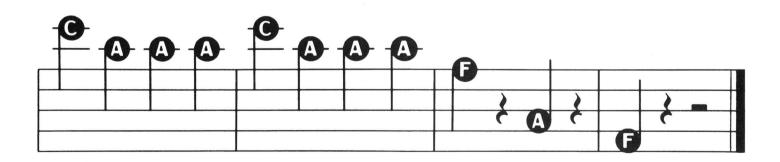

Voices of Spring

Registration 5
Rhythm: Waltz

By Johann Strauss

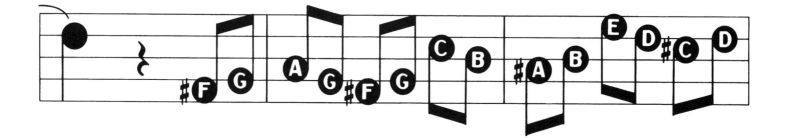

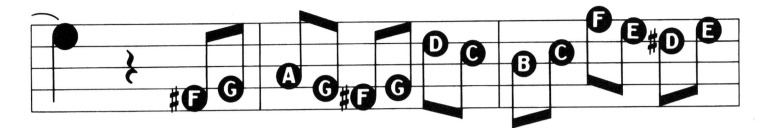

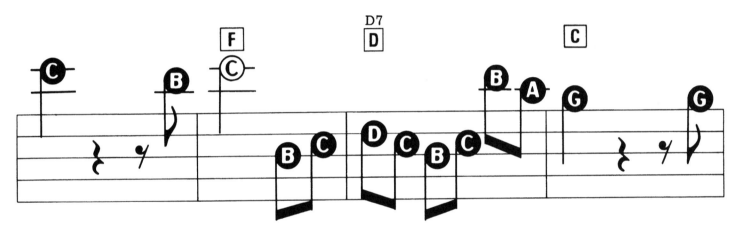

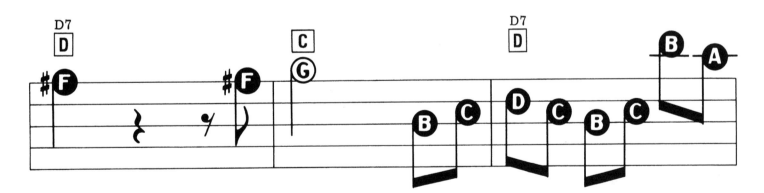

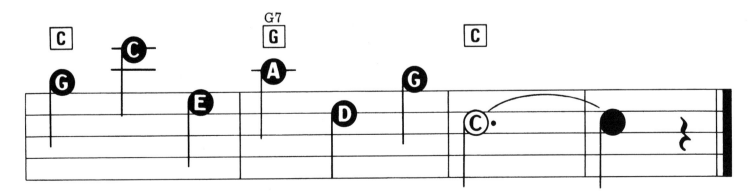

Waltz of the Flowers
from THE NUTCRACKER

Registration 9
Rhythm: Waltz

By Pyotr Il'yich Tchaikovsky

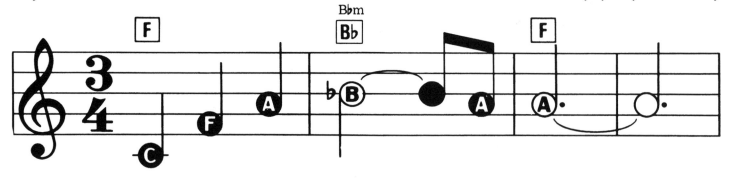

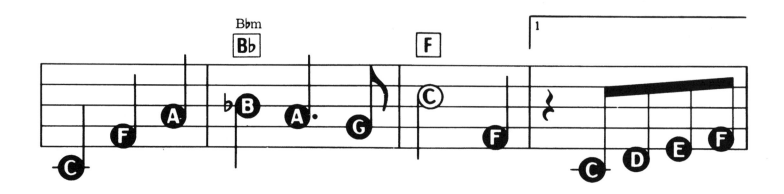

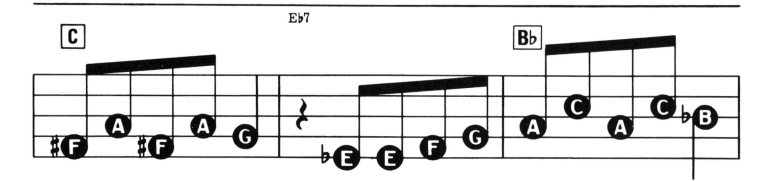

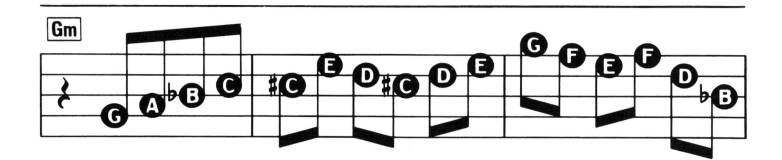

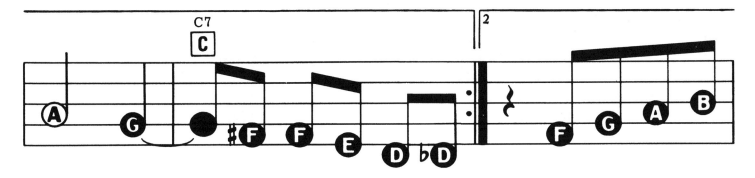

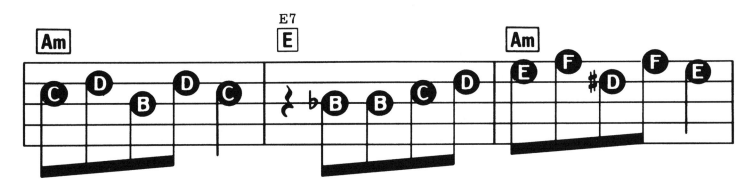

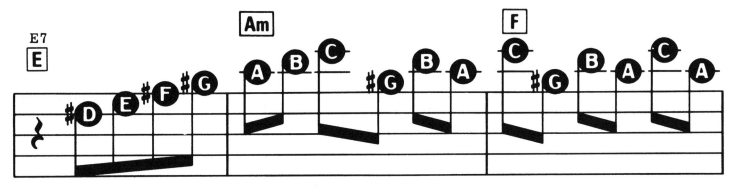

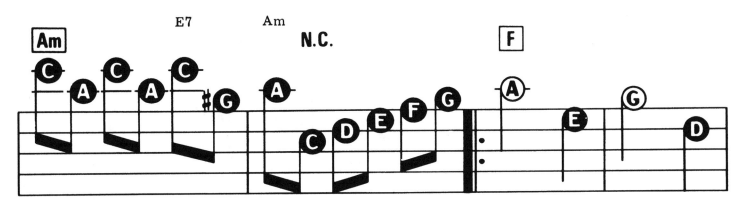

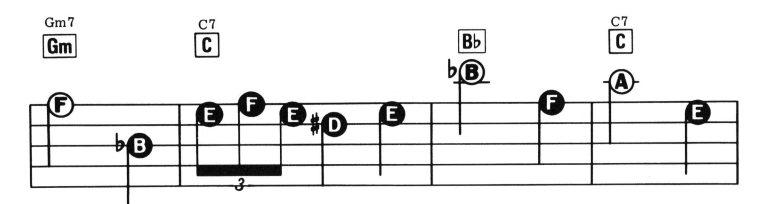

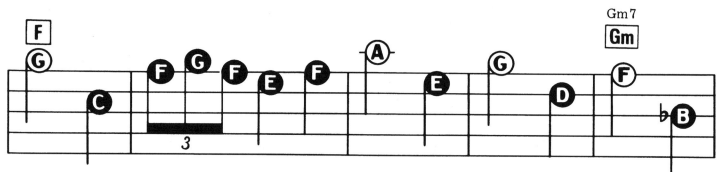

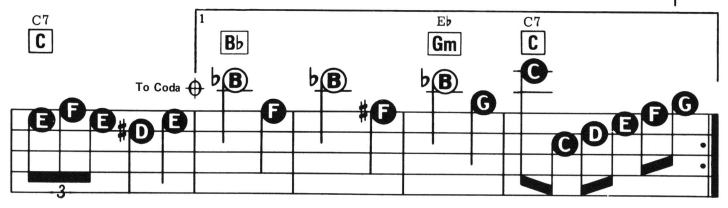

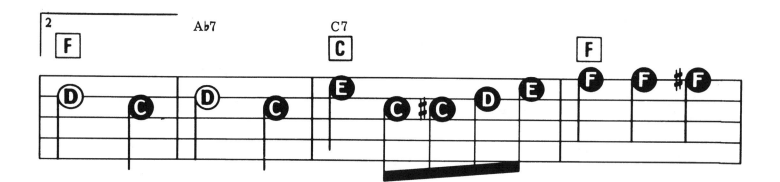

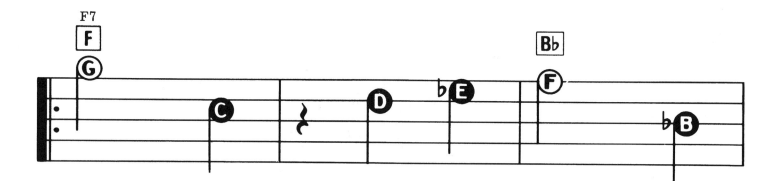

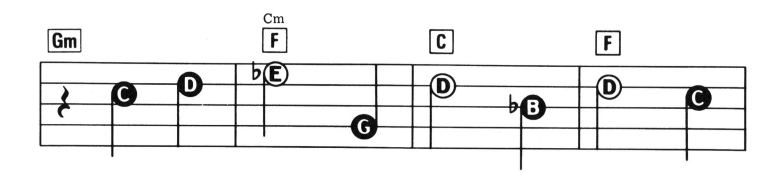

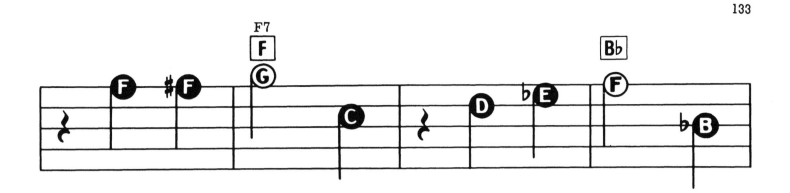

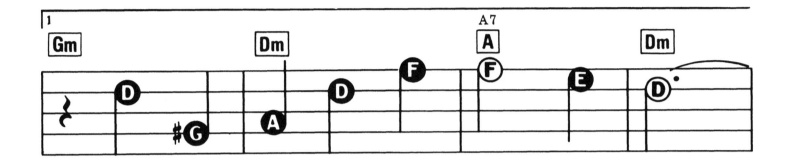

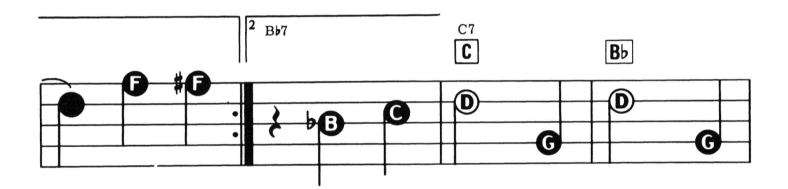

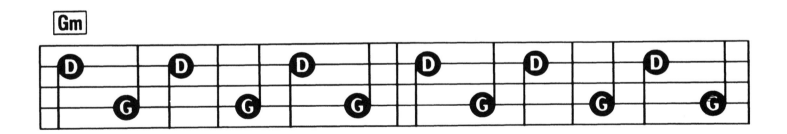

D.C. al Coda
(Return to beginning
Play to ⊕ and skip to Coda)

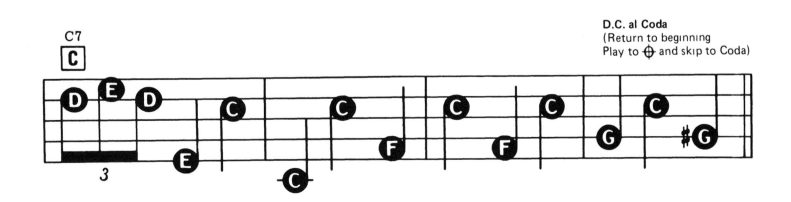

134

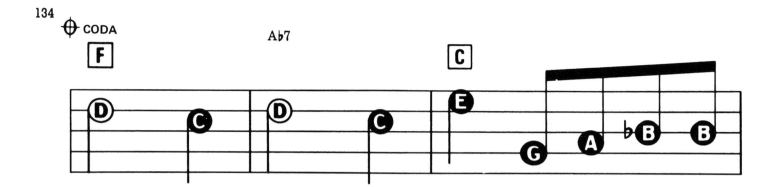

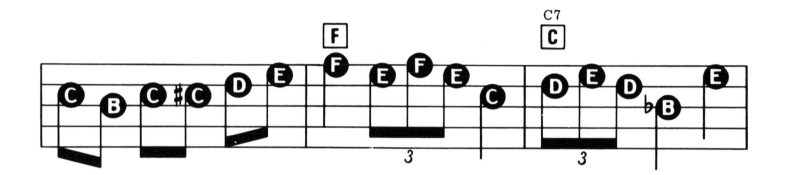

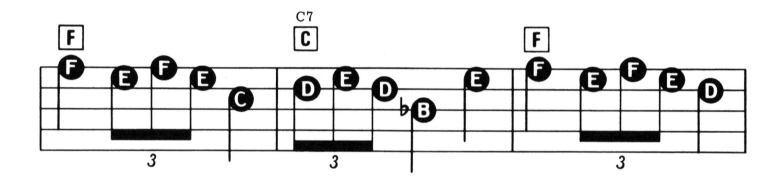

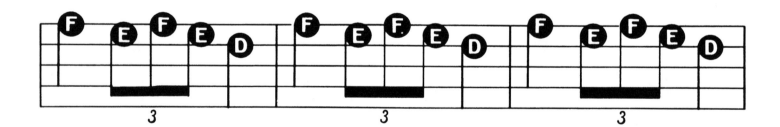

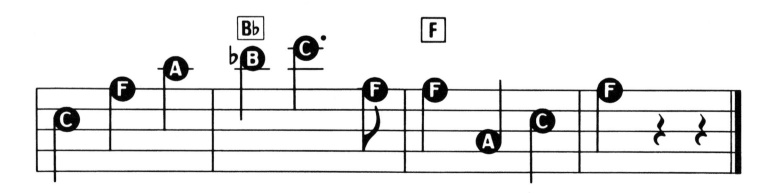

Wedding March
(Bridal Chorus)
from LOHENGRIN

Registration 6
Rhythm: None

By Richard Wagner

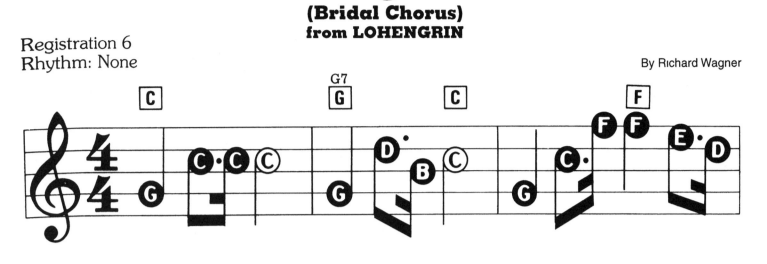

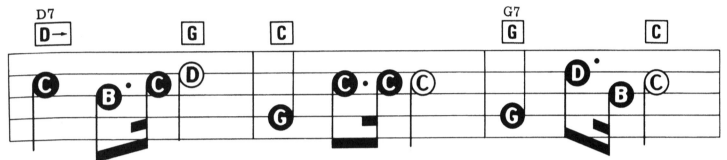

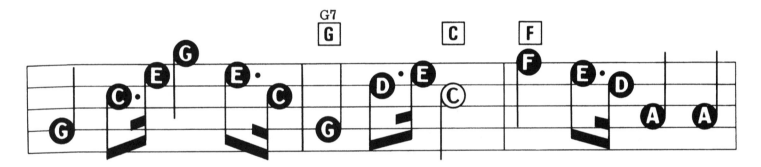

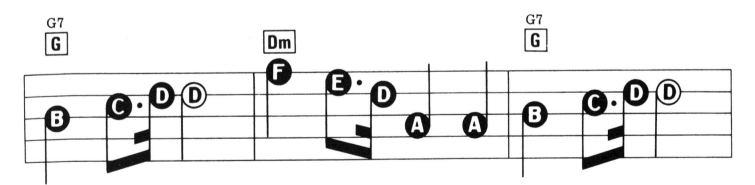

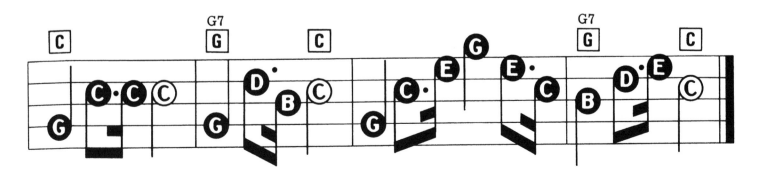

Registration Guide

- Match the Registration number on the song to the corresponding numbered category below. Select and activate an instrumental sound available on your instrument.

- Choose an automatic rhythm appropriate to the mood and style of the song. (Consult your Owner's Guide for proper operation of automatic rhythm features.)

- Adjust the tempo and volume controls to comfortable settings.

Registration

1	Mellow	Flutes, Clarinet, Oboe, Flugel Horn, Trombone, French Horn, Organ Flutes
2	Bright	Saxophones, Trumpet, Mute Trumpet, Synth Leads, Jazz/Gospel Organs
3	Guitars	Acoustic/Electric Guitars, Banjo, Mandolin, Dulcimer, Ukulele, Hawaiian Guitar
4	Strings	Violin, Viola, Cello, Fiddle, String Ensemble, Pizzicato, Organ Strings
5	Mallets	Vibraphone, Marimba, Xylophone, Steel Drums, Bells, Celesta, Chimes
6	Bellows	Accordion, French Accordion, Mussette, Harmonica, Pump Organ, Bagpipes
7	Liturgical	Pipe Organ, Hand Bells, Vocal Ensemble, Choir, Organ Flutes
8	Piano	Piano, Electric Piano, Honky Tonk Piano, Harpsichord, Clavi
9	Novelty	Melodic Percussion, Wah Trumpet, Synth, Whistle, Kazoo, Perc. Organ
10	Ensemble	Brass Section, Sax Section, Wind Ensemble, Full Organ, Theater Organ